✠ praise for *Sister Freaks* ✠

"I totally love *this book. These true stories—of young women who are sold out to God and willing to take on whatever He calls them to—just blew me away. Besides actually making me cry, they also challenged me to look more deeply into my own life and calling. I seriously recommend this book to anyone who truly wants to serve God. Really,* Sister Freaks *is awesome!"*
—Melody Carlson, author of *Diary of a Teenage Girl* and the True Colors series for teens

"Each person is asked to sacrifice something in life. Sister Freaks *is full of inspiring stories of both modern and biblical women who took courage and lived for what they believed. Rebecca St. James does an excellent job encouraging women to embrace the calling that God has on each of their lives, no matter what the sacrifice may be. This is imperative in seeing our younger generation, especially women, raised up to be the world-changing leaders they are destined to be. I highly recommend this book!"*
—Ron Luce, author of *Battle Cry for a Generation* and president, Teen Mania Ministries

sister freaks

STORIES OF WOMEN WHO GAVE UP EVERYTHING FOR GOD

Rebecca St. James

General Editor

WITH CONTRIBUTIONS FROM

Mary DeMuth

Elizabeth Jusino

Tracey Lawrence

Leigh McLeroy

Donna Wallace

WARNER
Faith®

NEW YORK BOSTON NASHVILLE

Out of respect for those involved, names of individuals have been changed.
Permission was granted to relate personal stories.

All Scripture quotations, unless otherwise indicated, are taken from
the *Holy Bible: New International Version*® NIV®. Copyright © 1973, 1978, 1984
by International Bible Society. Used by permission of Zondervan
Publishing House. All rights reserved.
Quotations noted NASB are from the *New American Standard Bible*®,
Copyright © 1960, 1962, 1963, 1968, 1971, 1972, 1973, 1975, 1977, 1988,
and 1995 by The Lockman Foundation, and are used by permission.
Quotations noted KJV are from the King James Version of the Bible.
Quotations noted NLT are from the *Holy Bible, New Living Translation*,
Copyright © 1996. Used by permission of Tyndale House Publishers, Inc.,
Wheaton, Illinois 60189. All rights reserved.

Warner Faith
Time Warner Book Group
1271 Avenue of the Americas, New York, NY 10020
Visit our Web site at www.warnerfaith.com

The Warner Faith name and logo are registered trademarks of
the Time Warner Book Group.

Book design by Fearn Cutler de Vicq

Printed in the United States of America
First Warner Faith printing: November 2005
10 9 8 7 6 5 4 3 2 1

Library of Congress Cataloging-in-Publication Data

St. James, Rebecca.
Sister freaks : stories of women who gave up everything for God /
Rebecca St. James.—1st ed.
p. cm.
ISBN 0-446-69560-2
1. Christian women—Biography. 2. Women missionaries—Biography.
3. Young women—Prayer-books and devotions—English. I. Title.
BR1713.S72 2005
270'.092'2—dc22 2005016213

This book is dedicated to all the young women
who have given it all to the Lord Jesus.
We'll see you in His presence!

⚜ contents ⚜

⚡ introduction ⚡

I grew up in Australia. Australians love hot tea. We have morning tea, afternoon tea, late-afternoon tea, and post-dinner tea. Some night owls like me might regularly enjoy a midnight decaf. Many Australians bring out the Old English teacups for their "cuppa." The younger set might sport a funky mug. But generally, the Australian tea break is a mild, sedate affair.

Watchman Nee once said, "Everywhere Jesus went, there was revolution. Everywhere I go, they serve tea."

I can relate. Sometimes it seems like everyone around me is nice and quiet and sedate—like we're all having a cup of tea. There's nothing wrong with that, of course. We all love Jesus; I just wonder sometimes if we're accomplishing something great for His kingdom.

If you're like me, you probably long to find those few who are different—the ones who are willing to take a strong stand for Jesus. It's not easy. I admire the *bold* women, the ones who stand up for something, the sisters strong enough to be considered "freaks" for the cause of Christ.

When you look at history, it's pretty clear that nobody was bolder than Jesus. He came down here to earth, even though He didn't have to, and sacrificed His life for each one of us. In doing that, He set an example of boldness. The Lord was so different from everyone else that the world couldn't help but notice Him. Two thousand years later, He is still the central figure in all history. I'm drawn to Him and His sacrifice and His example. The more I get to know Jesus, the more I want to be like Him.

But it's dangerous to live like the Lord. When He showed up, the world put Him to death. So we can't expect they're going to embrace us when we take a stand for God. In fact, we can expect to suffer, since great faith makes people uncomfortable. And that leads me to ask you: what sort of a stand do you want to take? What do you want to be known for?

Have you ever struggled with the sense that you're not strong enough, that you haven't done enough, or have your heart set on the wrong things? I have. But no matter how much I fail, I know God is right there, ready to strengthen me and help me become someone who is willing to take a stand. That's why I love these stories. Each one is about a young woman who took a great stand for God. Some of them are famous historical figures like Mary and Joan of Arc. Others are contemporary women you've probably never heard of. Each one has made an effort to change the world, even if it's in a small way. But every one held true to God, and they all inspire me to live a bigger, greater life.

If you use this book in your devotional reading, you'll find twelve weeks of stories—five per week—with a page for reflection at the end of each week, so you can explore what the Lord's leading is for your own life. As you read through these, I pray you'll see the world through His eyes and look for ways you can change it through His power.

One last word: the stories in this book have been crafted by several women writers who are themselves strong sisters in Christ. I want to thank them for helping put this project together, and I want to say a special "thank you" to all those who shared their stories with us. If I have to be considered a "Sister Freak" to stand with them, so be it. This is for all the Sister Freaks in the world who want more out of life than a cup of tea.

~Rebecca St. James

karen watson

NO REGRETS

Karen Watson entered a war zone because she loved Jesus. She knew the risks. News reports in early 2004 were riddled with American casualties in recently liberated Iraq. Car bombs blew up convoy trucks. Suicide bombers targeted civilians. Ambushes occurred weekly.

But a Scripture burned on Karen's heart—one that propelled her to Iraq: "Then I heard the voice of the Lord, saying, 'Whom shall I send, and who will go for Us?'" Her answer echoed Isaiah's: "Then I said, 'Here am I. Send me!'" (Isa. 6:8 NASB).

Karen had accepted Christ after experiencing severe grief as a teen. Her fiancé, her father, and her grandmother all died within a two-year period, and her pain had driven her into the arms of Jesus. Soon after, Karen took part in short-term mission trips, flying from Bakersfield, California, to El Salvador, Macedonia, Kosovo, and Greece. After those excursions, Karen knew she wanted to be a full-time missionary, despite the world climate.

Once accepted by the IMB (International Mission Board, a Southern Baptist missionary organization), she sold her home and car and submitted her resignation to the Kern County Sheriff's Department, where she had worked for eight years as a detention officer.

The IMB immediately sent Karen to Jordan to coordinate refugee relief during the war in Iraq. When the expected influx of refugees did not arrive, she was reassigned to Iraq. Then the UN building was bombed there, killing several civilians. Karen called home to California to say she was okay. She frequented the UN building but had not been inside the day of the bombing. After that day, however, she made it a point to call her family and supporters after every act of violence, just to assure them she was all right.

On March 15, 2004, Karen, along with several other missionaries, headed to Mosul, Iraq's third largest city. They were involved in humanitarian aid, developing a water purification system for the area. Partway through the missionaries' journey, Iraqi militants in a passing car assaulted them with automatic weapons and rocket-powered grenades.

When friends at home heard about the violent car ambush, they expected another satellite phone call. But this time Karen didn't call. She had died instantly, a casualty of bullet and shell fragment wounds.

Before she left for Iraq, Karen had discussed the risks with Roger Spradlin, one of her pastors from Valley Baptist Church in Bakersfield, California. "She was very, very brave, and she knew the risk of being in that part of the world," he says. "But she weighed that risk against the people's need for the gospel."

One of her friends related, "Karen was a real soldier in God's army and she will be greatly missed, but we know that she is now celebrating and worshiping the God she served."

Another friend noted, "Karen was the type who would

stand up for the Lord anywhere in the world. She felt the Lord Jesus was worth it."

After her death was confirmed, another pastor, Phil Neighbors, opened a letter she had written before she left for Iraq—to be opened if she were killed. It read:

March 7, 2003

Dear Pastor Phil and Pastor Roger,

You should only be opening this letter in the event of [my] death. When God calls there are no regrets. I tried to share my heart with you, my heart for the Nations. I wasn't called to a place. I was called to Him. To obey was my objective, to suffer was expected, His glory was my reward, His glory is my reward.

One of the most important things to remember right now is to preserve the work. I am writing this as if I am still working [in the mission field].

I thank you all so much for your prayers and support. Surely your reward in Heaven will be great. Thank you for investing in my life and spiritual well being. Keep sending missionaries out. Keep raising up fine pastors.

In regards to any service, keep it small and simple. Yes, simple. Just preach the gospel. If Jason Buss is available or his dad, have them sing a pretty song. Be bold and preach the life saving, life changing, forever eternal GOSPEL. Give glory and honor to our Father.

I once read in The Missionary Heart:

Care more than some think is wise.
Risk more than some think is safe.
Dream more than some think is practical.
Expect more than some think is possible.

I was called not to comfort or success but to obedience.
There is no joy outside of knowing Jesus and serving Him.
I love you two and my church family.

In His care,
Karen

Karen Watson spent her life for the cause of Jesus Christ among the nations, particularly one that appeared to be an enemy. People from that country took her life, yet her life continues on—as an ongoing testimony that God will expand His kingdom through those who dare to step outside of their comfort zones for His renown.

No one knows what Karen thought when she felt the bullets tear through her and the life drain from her body. But she lived her life without regret. Perhaps, as she grew closer to seeing Jesus' face, she recounted one of her favorite Psalms:

Though a host encamp against me,
My heart will not fear;
Though war arise against me,
In spite of this, I shall be confident.
One thing I have asked from the LORD, that I shall seek:
That I may dwell in the house of the LORD all the days
*   of my life,*
To behold the beauty of the LORD and to meditate in His
*   temple.*

(Psalm 27:3–4 NASB)

joan of arc
THE BRAVE SOLDIER

She rivals mythic characters such as Robin Hood and King Arthur, yet she was a real girl in history. Joan of Arc was born in Domrémy, a village in Lorraine, France, in January 1412. She was a common girl whose mother, Isabelle, trained her for the traditional female tasks of her day: cooking, cleaning, and tending sheep. She also learned her prayers from her mother, who nurtured her spiritually. Joan was particularly skilled in sewing and spinning.

Yet her life was to be lived out on a battlefield.

England had invaded northern France in 1417, and Joan experienced the devastation of the Hundred Years' War. Then, when this daughter of a peasant was about twelve years old, she began to hear a voice telling her she must save France from the English. If you've already heard this story, this news might not seem like very much. But consider this: a soldier in the fifteenth century protected the innocent; girls needed protection. A soldier wore armor; girls wore frilly dresses and bonnets. So for Joan to dream of taking part in anything other than the usual female tasks of the day was a huge contradiction.

The amazing thing is that Joan's father, Jacques d'Arc, once had a dream that his daughter was traveling with an army. Disturbed by such images, he told Joan's brothers but not his daughter. He was fearful of what the dream might mean, and he vowed to drown her if she ever became a soldier. Such a thing would disgrace the family.

Joan doesn't seem to have had a great attachment to her family. When the voice she heard intensified, she decided to leave her domestic life, pretending to go help her cousin, who was expecting a child. Her visions of Saints Catherine and Margaret, two early Christian martyrs, and Saint Michael the archangel, evoked her strong conviction that God was calling her to carry out a mission. After she left home, she never spoke to her family again.

Joan's behavior was radical and unacceptable. Why would a girl who had never traveled ten miles from her home leave it? Yet it is known that she asserted, "Since God commanded it, had I had a hundred fathers and a hundred mothers, had I been born a king's daughter, I should have departed."

Naturally, her claims caused great speculation. Though during this time mysticism was popular in the church, it was still questionable for someone to claim to "hear voices." But her passion was sincere; even though Joan never experienced peace in her homeland, she longed for France to be restored and a king to be crowned to lead her country. However far-fetched her desires seemed, she followed them because she believed them to be of God.

At the age of seventeen, Joan boldly approached Robert de Baudricourt, the lord of her local district, as if she were his equal and asked for her own army. At first Baudricourt was skeptical, but her persistence impressed him, and he finally believed that God had sent her. He granted her stunning request.

Soon Joan found herself on a journey to meet Charles, the son of Charles VI, who she believed would be the next king. Mysteriously, Charles gave her his favor and support, but he knew that in the current political climate, and with Joan claiming a calling from God, Joan would also need the support of the church. So he arranged for the doctors and archbishops of the church to interrogate Joan. They found nothing heretical about her visions and respected her simplicity and honesty. She passed their examination.

Joan was given a suit of armor made just for her. There she was, a domesticated peasant girl adorned in clothes of war. She was about to be a commander over men. A white linen banner was given to her with an image of the Trinity and two angels, which would become the sign by which Joan would be recognized. The banner read "Of the Party of the King of Heaven." This was her public declaration of her divine calling to save her beloved country.

Then, with her four thousand men Joan faced the English in Orleans. The first night in the field, she lay weary and bruised from the weight of her heavy armor. One can only imagine how she felt, knowing she was finally fulfilling God's call on her life.

Naïve, but full of determination, Joan soon found herself fighting battles within the ranks of her own army. Many of the men did not take her seriously and saw her more as a mascot than a military leader. But Joan knew she was much more than an ornament of war. Being a female did not limit what she believed God would accomplish through her. Despite internal strife and Joan's naïveté, the French were able to conquer the

English at Orleans, and Charles was crowned king. It seemed God's grace was working on their behalf.

Because of Joan's unconquerable spirit and ability to face the impossible, her men were strengthened and inspired. Her mission had been successful. Joan could then have returned home to live in peace, but she continued to choose the life of a soldier.

Despite all Joan's victories in the field, as she worked to recapture Paris, English soldiers captured her in 1430 and she was tried by bribed officials as a heretic. They condemned her claims to have heard from God as demonic. Enduring eight months in prison, she was taunted by English soldiers, chained to her bed, and forbidden to take Communion. She was found guilty of idolatry both for hearing voices and for wearing men's clothing.

On May 30, 1431, at Rouen, she walked in chains, silenced by the jeering, savage crowds who wanted to witness her death. Joan requested that a crucifix be placed in front of her as she was tied to a stake. Repeatedly she cried out, "Jesus!" Her passing was slow and agonizing, as executioners had been instructed to keep her at a distance from the flames to torture her. Focusing on the cross, Joan resigned herself to death.

Joan's partly charred body was shown to the crowd in order to prove that she was indeed a woman. Then the body was completely burned. Heretics at the time could not receive a Christian burial, and Joan's remains were cast into the Seine River.

The brave soldier died alone at nineteen. Legends soon followed. Some said they saw a dove swoop down over her at the stake. Others said her heart would not burn and remained in the ashes. Whatever legends continue to surround Joan of

Arc's controversial life, her single-minded devotion to her calling was clear.

In the Middle Ages, it was unheard of for a woman to mark history outside of her traditional role. Women were viewed as objects of men's desires, not as vessels the Lord might use to change history. Yet indeed, Joan of Arc did change history, despite the odds.

For our struggle is not against flesh and blood, but against the rulers, against the authorities, against the powers of this dark world and against the spiritual forces of evil in the heavenly realms.

(Ephesians 6:12)

---

anna Mikelson

A SMOOTH AND STEADY PACE

Olympic silver medalist Anna Mikelson had long envisioned herself competing in the world's most famous games—but not on the water, and not with a team of seven other female athletes. Anna began running track when she was five years old, and she imagined crossing the Olympic finish line among other runners. God had other ideas.

Raised in the Seattle, Washington, area, Anna competed in track, cross-country, and basketball in high school. Her father, brother, and sister-in-law all ran for the University of Washington Huskies, and Anna hoped to follow in their footsteps. There was just one problem: every track and field coach who looked at her height, weight, and race times believed that she had maxed out in her sport. Although her times were good, they weren't certain to improve a great deal.

But Anna's high-school cross-country coach knew the rowing coach at the University of Washington, and Anna was invited to join the crew. The coaches at Washington took one look at her tall, athletic build and said, "You would be really good at this." Wanting to believe in what the Huskies envisioned for her, Anna walked onto a national powerhouse rowing team, earning a scholarship the next year. "They sought me out and taught me what to do with a big oar," she says simply.

Anna proved to be a quick study in her new sport. A four-time NCAA national champion rower, two-time College Rowing Coaches Association academic All-American, and three-time Pacific-10 academic All-American, she was the recipient of both NCAA and Pacific-10 postgraduate scholarships. As a collegian she rowed on the "women's eight" national teams in 2001 and 2002, placing fourth and first respectively in the world championships, and graduated from the University of Washington in 2002 with a degree in communications and a 3.6 GPA.

In August of 2004, Anna and her teammates rowed to a second-place finish in the Olympic Games in Athens, Greece. In their qualifying heat, the women set a new world record of 5:56 for the women's eight—a two-thousand-meter race with an eight-woman crew. In the final, they battled two-time reigning Olympic champions from Romania and were well pleased with the first medal for the United States in that event in twenty years.

Today Anna divides her time between continuing to train on the water in Seattle and working for the University of Washington Athletic Department and the National Rowing Association. She also speaks to corporate executives and students of all ages about team building and motivation. "We use our boat as an example for teamwork," she says, "and we encourage younger kids just to have fun and be healthy." She hopes one day to work in athletic administration, but whatever the future holds, it is sure to include a constant that she has pursued with a passion equal to her sport: building relationships to share the love of Christ.

"In high school I was discipled by a woman in my church who worked with our youth group," says Anna. "She really made a difference in my life and is still a significant person to me today. Her example caused me to want to do for others what she has done for me." As a sophomore at Washington, Anna was living in a Christian house, but God was growing in her a love for her rowing teammates. "I wanted to reach out to them, but it's really hard to apply your faith in all areas of your life—to have it fully integrated into your world and not compartmentalized into one tiny little section."

Soon she started attending meetings of Athletes in Action (AIA), a ministry of Campus Crusade that was active on the U of W campus. Together with an AIA staff person, she started a Bible study. She continued to nurture small groups as an intern and later a volunteer for Campus Crusade at Princeton University.

"So much of my sport and my life are about relationships," she says. "I've loved rowing with these seven women. We're not just fellow athletes who train and compete together. We're women who can also pray for each other and share life together."

Anna is currently discipling two other rowers, a process she admits is time intensive and deeply relational. "There's a fine balance of feeling each person out and determining what level of communication and interaction she is open to," she says. "I want everyone to know the great joy in Christ—but the privilege of sharing that comes over time by caring about people no matter where they're at, asking questions to know them better, and whenever possible, using Christ as an example."

Anna's message is simple, and it's straight from the pages of her own life: God has a plan for you. "I have always thought the pop culture ideal has a quick appeal," she says. "I wanted to have a made-for-TV life, but I guess I always knew it wasn't that easy. I understood that the things I focused on—sports, school, family, and friends—were the foundation for a great life if Christ was my center. He made them have a deeper meaning, and now I would say that my life is like the perfect movie because God is my Director."

Even though she may not line up exactly with the world's standard for feminine appeal, Anna's comfortable with being "a tall, strong woman." She explains, "The world tells us that our performance, plus what others think about us, equals who we are. But that's not true. We are who God says we are. He establishes our identity, and out of that will flow our performance and our relationships, not the other way around."

Refusing to be satisfied with her present set of skills, Anna is adding another challenge to her agenda: she is learning to row sculls instead of shells and becoming adept with two oars instead of just one. With those added abilities, she'll be able to compete for any rowing spot on the 2008 Olympic team.

But her focus is flexible. "We'll see what happens," she says cheerfully. "God may have other plans. It's like the verse says: "'For I know the plans I have for you,'" declares the LORD, "plans for welfare and not for calamity to give you a future and a hope'" [Jer. 29:11 NASB]. I'm taking it one day at a time, one year at a time. We'll see what He has in store. I don't view life as a series of big moments—even moments like winning an Olympic medal. It's more about the process for me."

For Anna, it's one long, smooth, and steady race. She's rowing strong, and she's sure to finish well.

Do you not know that in a race all the runners run, but only one gets the prize? Run in such a way as to get the prize.

(1 Corinthians 9:24)

shannon wright

A CHANGE OF PLANS

Shannon Wright jokingly confesses that growing up as a Southern Baptist in Texas, she wasn't sure Presbyterians were even Christians. Today twenty-seven-year-old Shannon serves as a deacon in her inner-city, evangelical Presbyterian church. And although she planned to move away from her home state of Texas after graduation from Wellesley, she's returned there to pursue a calling that wasn't quite what she had in mind either.

Shannon's dream was the excitement and prestige of a literary career. "At seventeen," she says, "I imagined myself at twenty-seven as a writer in New York, wearing a little black dress and dropping witty one-liners to the worshipful crowd."

But after her sophomore year in college, as she was pursuing her carefully mapped-out plan of becoming a journalist, Shannon's direction changed. The newspaper summer job that she had lined up fell through, and instead Shannon found herself answering the call of a homeless shelter to run a summer program for kids. She calls the job a "baptism by fire" introduction to issues of race and social justice that she'd only read about before: "For the first time I saw how crushing poverty can be to the spirit, and how ugly the physical manifestations of racism are. But at the same time, I was introduced to children who were bright and resilient and funny and savvy in the face of it all, who demonstrated unshakable faith and irrepressible spirits."

It was also the first time Shannon learned how it felt to be in the minority, where her hair and skin color were the exception and where she had to acclimate to someone else's culture. The hard questions she began to ask about where her life might be heading were uncomfortable, but she says they were unmistakably "the probing of the Spirit, leading me slowly off the road I had been groomed for." Instead of worldly success and respect and influence—"the kind of stuff your dad can brag about on the golf course"—Shannon felt a pull toward something she knew would "challenge me every day, show up every weakness I had, play on all my vulnerabilities, invest me with responsibility which I don't always discharge well, and put me right in the midst of the salvation drama."

While she'd planned on garnering publishing successes and accolades, Shannon now recounts a different kind of reality: she deals each day with AIDS babies, people struggling with drug relapses, abused children, and the overt racism frequently directed at them. And for inspiration, she reads Dietrich Bonhoeffer and Saint Francis of Assisi, Martin Luther King and Dorothy Day.

Instead of writing scintillating pieces for the mass market, she writes letters to a drug-addicted mother who has lost her children and is dying herself of AIDS, to say: "You are loved. You have a Shepherd. Your life is not a waste. Your children will be cared for. You are a daughter of the King, and He is present in your suffering and He thinks you are beautiful, and He can still redeem you and bring you to glory."

This young woman who imagined herself as a media mover and shaker is these days growing into "an imperfect vessel that gets to be a conduit of perfect grace." And Shannon says it's the reason she shows up every day. "You get to stand with them in the trenches," she says. "You tell the stories of the miracles because we know they do happen, and you don't pretend it doesn't break your heart, because some days, it does."

In spring of 2004, Shannon received an unexpected invitation to be the commencement speaker for a small Christian high school in another state. She spent a lot of time thinking about what to say to young people who were just a few years younger than herself—what sorts of words might ring true to eager eighteen-year-olds going off in pursuit of their dreams. Her audience received her words with more than a little discomfort. Her speech's frankness and honesty were stripped of the usual "the world is your oyster" platitudes. But within a few days it was making its way across the Internet to a broader audience than she ever imagined.

What did she say that caused such a stir? "Fear not." She urged the graduating class of 2004 not to be afraid of failing, of disappointing people, or of their own unique callings and paths.

"Don't be afraid of the world," she told them. "You have nothing to fear from the world. Christ has already told you He has overcome it. Engage it. Understand it. Know why people think the way they think, what they care about, what they're afraid of, what makes them laugh, and what keeps them up at three in the morning. Remember the first Bible verse you ever learned: 'For God so loved the world.' God does love the world, and the sign of a God-lover is to love the things He loves."

She also implored them not to be afraid of the church, in what she described as "all of its multi-hued, chaotic, messy glory." She assured them that as they came to know more believers of other stripes, "there will be days when you think, *God has no standards and no taste.* Other days, of course, this is what gives you hope for yourself." Instead of being fenced in behind denominational boundaries and caught up in theological squabbles, Shannon asked her audience not to be afraid of other worship styles or different denominational norms.

So, while she's not communicating in quite the way she might have planned at seventeen, this young writer/social activist/church leader is finding her voice and helping others find theirs. And she's not so worried anymore about what others might think: "It can be the most liberating thing in the world to refuse to be held hostage by the expectations of others, even when those others are incredibly loving and well-meaning people," Shannon says. "Ultimately, the call of Christ is one that only you can discern. So go ahead and disappoint some people and show yourself that it won't kill you.

"I'm still standing. Disappointment hasn't made me wither up and die. I stay as close to the call of Christ as I can, I start over when I mess up, and I get over it when people aren't happy with me. And I'm a bit freer than I was at seventeen—not all the way there, to be sure, but a little farther down the road."

Always give yourself fully to the work of the Lord, because you know that your labor in the Lord is not in vain.

(1 Corinthians 15:58)

danielle, tara, crystal, and kimberly
A HOUSE OF HOPE

When thirteen-year-old Danielle stepped into the spotlight at a national women's conference in San Antonio, Texas, it was probably a good thing she couldn't see the ten thousand or so women in the Alamodome waiting to hear what she had to say. But her voice was calm and clear, and when she finished speaking, the auditorium erupted with applause and her audience stood to its feet.

This is what she told them: "Hi, my name is Danielle. I was born and raised in Orlando, Florida. I've been in House of Hope for nine months now. My life was pretty good until I was ten years old and my grandpa died. After that, my parents got divorced, and because of it I had to switch schools a lot. My grades dropped from A's to F's. Then, at the age of eleven, I started smoking marijuana, dating older guys, drinking, and going to clubs. Then, because I wanted to look like my friends, I started selling my body to buy new clothes. What I didn't buy I shoplifted. I got involved in gangs, witchcraft, and pornography. I ran away several times and was arrested. Finally, I was brought to House of Hope."

As Danielle spoke, the room was quieter than it had been all weekend. "Soon after I got to House of Hope, I accepted Jesus Christ as my Lord and Savior. I was actually baptized in October. I am a 'born-again virgin.' My family is being restored, which I thought would never happen, and I learned that Jesus Christ is going to love, accept, and forgive me no matter what.

"I want to be brave and courageous like Queen Esther in the Bible. I am taking the chance of losing my popularity just as she did to help others, to help save my generation." Danielle then asked her sisters in the Lord, "Would you please pray that I keep making good choices?" And she thanked them for listening to her story.

House of Hope was established in 1985 by Sara Trollinger, a former schoolteacher who believed God was leading her to begin a ministry to troubled teens. She felt she should provide a place where they could learn responsibility and respect for authority and experience the healing and restoring touch of God on their lives. Nearly twenty years later, House of Hope has been instrumental in changing thousands of lives. Sara's goal is to have a House of Hope in every major city in America by 2010.

Young girls like Danielle are not just quitting drugs and learning to live sexually pure lives again. They're finding Christ and finding their voices—and speaking boldly about how their lives have turned around.

Tara grew up with an alcoholic mother and a critical stepfather who was also physically abusive. When she was seven years old, she was molested by one of his friends—something both parents denied ever happened. By the time she was barely a teenager, Tara had begun to smoke, have sex, and poison her body with cocaine and other drugs.

"I began to fight with my mom over everything," says Tara, "taking advantage of her when she was drunk and not listening to what she told me to do. I was a mess and she was a mess. I was confused and full of shame, and I hated myself for the mistakes I had made."

At House of Hope, Tara met Christ, received counseling, and began to rebuild her relationship with her mom. She says simply, "House of Hope saved my life. My mom and I are getting the tools we need to survive in this world, and I'm keeping myself now for the man God has for me." Tara's favorite verse is Psalm 9:9: "The LORD is a refuge for the oppressed, / a stronghold in times of trouble." And she hasn't just memorized it, she's living it: "Now I run to Jesus when I'm in trouble," she says. "He is my stronghold."

Crystal, too, found a refuge at House of Hope. She grew up in church, but by the time she was fourteen her life was slipping out of control. "My father was on drugs and was a very abusive man," she explains. "My mother remarried a man who molested me when I was seven years old. Finally the anger inside of me began to explode.

"I started skipping school, got into the wrong crowd, and began sneaking out of the house. My grades went from B's to F's. One night when I was drinking I lost my virginity to a stranger. I was full of shame. I began taking Ecstasy, got alcohol poisoning, and was hospitalized. I was arrested for shoplifting, and that's when my mom took me to House of Hope."

What Crystal found there was Jesus. "I didn't realize before who He really was," she says. "At House of Hope I made the decision to dedicate my life to Him, and already I see changes. I'm still dealing with a lot, but I'm relying on God to help me get through it. I know He is changing me day by day.

As the Bible says in Isaiah 54:4, I will not be put to shame, or humiliated or disgraced for the mistakes I made in my youth. God has erased them from my life and is making me into a new person. He won't take me out of the temptations of this world, but He will protect me and work with me so I can make good choices. I know He'll take care of me as long as I trust Him."

Kimberly grew up a pastor's daughter, and her parents were very strict. "I was not even allowed to wear jeans to youth group," she says. "I felt like an oddball." But when Kimberly was thirteen, her father left the church and her family has never returned. "My world fell apart," she remembers. "It was hard to see God as a loving Father when my own father had let me down. So I started looking for the love I needed in all the wrong places: alcohol, drugs, and friends who pulled me down. That's when I lost my virginity."

Kimberly hit bottom when she was molested by a relative who warned that if she told anyone, he would kill her. Her mother took her to House of Hope to see if healing was possible. "There I found the real Jesus for myself," Kimberly explains. "I like the verse in Isaiah that says God's love has delivered my soul from the pit and He has cast all my sins behind His back [Isa. 38:17]. I have forgiven the people who hurt me. And God has blessed me with the talent to sing, so I want to use my voice to praise Jesus forever."

Danielle, Tara, Crystal, and Kimberly have hope for the future. They are all grateful for the way God met them where they were and saved them just in time. And they want to tell their stories to other girls who may be wondering if God is big enough to save them.

They know He is.

*Therefore if anyone is in Christ, he is a new creation; the old
has gone, the new has come!*

(2 Corinthians 5:17)

WEEK ONE JOURNAL

—◆—

⊷ In what ways is the mind-set of a servant different from the mind-set of the world?

⊷ Why do you think God designed us to live this way?

⊷ What kinds of challenges would you expect to face if servanthood became your lifestyle?

⊷ What would be some of the possible rewards?

⊷ What Bible verse or passage of Scripture has been most meaningful to you this week? Why?

crystal woodman
GET ME OUT ALIVE

C rystal Woodman's biggest concern that Tuesday morning was her physics test. She hadn't studied, and she
needed every free minute during the day to cram. When lunch
period started, she convinced her friends, Seth and Sara, to
come with her to the library instead of going off campus as
they usually did.

She had been actively involved in church and youth group
as a child, but in high school Crystal had turned away from
God to get involved in the party scene. After a few years of
trying to be "cool" by experimenting with drugs, alcohol, and
boys, Crystal began to see how empty her life was and went
back to church. Not entirely committed to either lifestyle, she
swung back and forth between the party kids and the church
kids, drawn to the deep relationships she saw in Christians like
Seth and Sara but also craving the popularity of the "in"
crowd.

The three friends pretended not to notice the librarian's
glare and chatted as they found an empty table. Instead of
studying, they joked around with a camera for a few minutes,

enjoying each other's company and the memories of prom the weekend before.

Slowly, they began to notice sounds and movements outside the library. Seth looked out the window, but the stream of students leaving the school looked like the usual lunch crowd. No one seemed to be paying much attention until a teacher ran into the library, screaming, "There are boys outside with guns and bombs. They're shooting students!"

Crystal searched for an explanation: It was a senior prank. It was a student's video project. Those were firecrackers exploding in the hallway. After all, nothing bad could happen there. They were in Littleton, Colorado, an upper-middle-class suburb of housing developments, parks, and strip malls. People didn't get shot there.

But it was April 20, 1999, and people were being shot at Columbine High School. As the sounds drew closer, Crystal watched a terrified classmate stumble into the library, clutching his bleeding shoulder. This was no prank. There was no time to escape. Crystal, Seth, and Sara took cover in the only place they could, under a library table. Seth pulled Crystal's head to his chest to protect her and whispered, "Start praying. I don't know what's happening. God is the only one who can get us through."

Two boys with guns entered the library. Eric Harris and Dylan Klebold, seniors at Columbine, began moving around the room, randomly shooting their classmates.

Crystal's face was hidden in Seth's shirt, but she remembers the sounds, smells, and feelings of the next few minutes. Gunshots and pipe bombs exploded around her, shattering glass and mixing with students' frightened cries and the angry voices of the killers. She smelled the smoke from the pipe bombs and felt the floor shake with every explosion.

The voices drew nearer, and Crystal realized, *It's my turn to die*. She heard a gunshot just a few feet away—a boy under the next table was killed merely because he wore glasses. For the first time, she thought she would not leave the Columbine library alive.

Crystal began to pray. "Okay, God, if You're real, get me out of here alive. I will give You my life forever. I'll quit partying. I will do anything. Just get me out of here. I didn't understand then. I do now. It all makes sense now."

One of the killers shoved in a library chair, and it hit Crystal's arm. They had reached her table. But even as she thought about dying, a voice in Crystal's mind told her, "God's going to get you out. You have a story to tell. God's going to get you out."

The two shooters began talking to each other. They had run out of ammunition, and their extra bag of bombs and bullets was in the hallway. Without even looking under Crystal's table, they left the library.

As soon as Eric and Dylan left, the surviving students began to leave through a fire escape. They knew the killers had just gone to reload; they would come back. In the instant before she left the library, Crystal looked around. "It was the first time I had seen the room. Everything had been shot up— the computers, the windows, the books—and little fires had been started from the pipe bombs. I saw the bodies of my classmates on the floor . . . and I knew that they were dead."

Crystal and the other survivors in the library ran together out of the school. Not sure how many shooters there were or whether they were watching, Crystal and the other kids took shelter behind a police car parked just outside.

Eventually, police officers took everyone farther away from the school. Crystal was separated from Seth and Sara and started to weep uncontrollably. "Everything I had known for sixteen years—my innocence, my security, my safety—was just stripped away from me. I didn't know what I had just seen; I hadn't processed it all."

Crystal joined the chaos, throngs of students wandering through the nearby park and shopping center, looking for phones to call parents or friends. It would take hours before everyone was reunited and the names of the dead were confirmed. Crystal walked across a field with Craig Scott while he looked for his sister, Rachel. They would later find out she was the first person murdered, shot just outside the building. Crystal would hear students telling the story of a classmate killed in a different part of the library after she affirmed her faith in Christ, without knowing right away that it was Cassie Bernall, a member of Crystal's youth group.

She eventually found a phone and called her father, who met her near the school. She filled out police reports and eventually went home for a tearful reunion with her mother and brother.

Even in her pain, Crystal remembered her promise to God, and she stepped forward again and again to tell her story. She quickly became the unofficial spokesperson for the Columbine students. She was interviewed on *Good Morning America, The Today Show,* CNN, and all of the Denver area news outlets. Wracked with depression and plagued by nightmares, Crystal wouldn't speak to anyone for weeks unless it was in an interview, but she found comfort in telling the world about how God saved her.

Over the coming weeks, as she worked through her own emotions, Crystal began speaking to groups—local churches at first, and then rallies, youth conferences, school assemblies, festivals, press conferences, and retreats. She became a living testimony of God's promise in 2 Corinthians 12:9: "My grace is sufficient for you, for my power is made perfect in weakness." God took Crystal's damaged, wounded spirit—the one that had seen so much pain—and used it to help others heal. Later, traveling to war-torn Kosovo with Operation Christmas Child (an outreach of Samaritan's Purse), Crystal met children who live every day with violence like that at Columbine. That event, coupled with others, led her to dedicate her life to speaking.

Now twenty-one and married, Crystal Woodman Miller continues to retell the story of her brush with death as a way to share the positive things that come from tragedy. She often quotes Genesis 50:20 when she speaks, a verse that so accurately describes her life and ministry: "You intended to harm me, but God intended it for good to accomplish what is now being done, the saving of many lives."

Crystal knows there are cruel and scary things in this world. But she knows also there is One who is stronger, and she is putting her faith in Him.

I tell you the truth, whoever hears my word and believes him who sent me has eternal life and will not be condemned; he has crossed over from death to life.

(John 5:24)

ʃara

GIRL ON THE RUN

It all started with simple curiosity. Tara, a twelve-year-old Islamic girl, found herself intrigued by some Bible curriculum she had ordered from an advertisement in the local Pakistani paper. Tara was from a prominent, strict Muslim family. She knew there were no options when it came to religion. In her father's eyes, there was no other religion but Islam.

But Tara was still drawn to what she was reading. Secretly, for two years, she studied every book of the Bible and finally completed the course. She was amazed at how much information the free curriculum provided. Soon after completing the study, she was sent a Bible with her name inscribed on it. Tara knew what would happen if she were caught with a Bible.

A year later, Tara completed her tenth year of school with high honors and was invited to participate in a comparative religion course in Iran. She eagerly accepted, but her family accompanied her.

There, she met a Christian for the first time. He was openly praying in a nearby courtyard. He invited her to a church service. Tara told her brother about the incident and pleaded with him to let her attend. She thought it would help with her research, she said, and finally she convinced him.

Tara entered the church, soaking in the thrilling, new experience. She recognized some of the words in the songs from reading the Bible. The sermon was about prayer, and the minister encouraged anyone with a need to come forward. A man walked up with a crippled child, asking for prayer. Tara couldn't believe that Christians could approach God like that and just ask for healing. Despite her skepticism, she witnessed the young girl beginning to move. She was healed!

The church began to sing praises to the Lord. Tara was awestruck. The young girl walked over to Tara and said, "Emmanuel." Afraid and unsure of what was happening, Tara was determined to find out more about this Christian faith. She went back home to read her Bible to find more answers. Yet she knew she needed to talk to other Christians to fully understand. So, she surreptitiously slipped out to attend a church service in her hometown.

Afterward, Tara had more questions than ever and went to meet the pastor. She thought it would be safe to talk openly with him, but she was wrong. The pastor grew more and more uncomfortable with Tara's tenacity and finally contacted her father, telling him of her private visits.

Her father was enraged to discover the truth about Tara. His once-favored daughter had betrayed him. He angrily ordered her to her room, cursing at her. Later, realizing how out of control his emotions were, he went into Tara's room to apologize. There, he found her weeping, reading her Bible. Repulsed by this, he struck her repeatedly, leaving her bruised and curled up in pain. Never had her father treated her that way before.

A few days later, her father apologized for his behavior. He and Tara's brother made arrangements for her to marry, thinking that would take care of her interest in Christianity. But Tara shuddered at the thought of getting married—she was only sixteen. "No, Daddy, I do not want to marry. I'm too young. Who is he? What is his religion?"

Tara had asked an unpardonable question. She had exposed her acceptance of other faiths. Her father was then convinced his daughter really had converted to Christianity. He and her brother angrily pummeled her with whatever they could find in the room—the beautiful crystal lamps that once decorated her princess-like room, electric cords, and a rod from her closet. "Either you marry this Muslim man, or you die here alone. If you are a Christian, there is no place for you in this city."

Tara's beating left her bleeding in her room, fading in and out of consciousness for a few days. She knew she had to make a choice. When she was able, she gathered a small travel bag with a bit of money and her passport and escaped out her bedroom window. Although she was sore, stiff, and heartbroken, she set out to learn more about the God of the Bible.

Tara's life on the run began. She first stopped at a city several hours from her home. There, through a church, she met an uncle she never knew about who had become a Christian back in the 1950s, when it was still legal to convert. He was a pastor, and Tara's father had disowned him. Through him, the Lord provided safety and a place where Tara could ground her faith at the beginning of what would be a very long journey.

Tara quickly learned to trust her uncle and brought all of her questions about God to him. She finally learned what *Emmanuel* meant. She felt ready to pray for God's forgiveness and make

Him Lord of her life. She could then live with the assurance that Emmanuel—"God with us"—was in fact with *her*.

Soon, it became unsafe for Tara to live with her uncle anymore. Her father wanted to kill Tara and had learned of her whereabouts. Tearfully, she knew she had to leave her uncle. Arrangements were made for her to live with a pastor's family in another distant city.

There, she was not allowed to come out of her room, for fear her brothers or father would find her. She spent many lonely days crying and trying to focus her attention on prayer and study. She knew if she went out in public, she would jeopardize her safety as well as that of the pastor's family.

Finally, the pastor let her leave her room. She then went to work as the church secretary. The pastor knew Tara's history and allowed her to minister to the covert Muslim converts. Tara began to understand how her testimony would strengthen others to follow Christ. She was able to live safely with this family for several years, baptizing former Muslims and Hindus and boldly evangelizing.

But one day, Tara ran into her cousin. She recognized him immediately. She quickly turned and started to walk away.

"Wait! I want to speak with you!" he called out.

She felt panic and fear run through her body and hailed a taxi. Once again, Tara was on the run, unsure of where God would take her next.

Later, she phoned her adopted family to tell them where she was. Tara was able to go back to them. But a church member, who was jealous of her beauty and strong faith, turned her in to the CID, Pakistan's intelligence organization. Once again, she found herself crying out to God, Emmanuel, to save her from death.

Despite her circumstances, Tara's faith continued to grow, and she knew God was using her life to help others. Danger was inevitable but she had made her choice—she was a disciple of Christ. Tara faced more threats, more betrayals, yet God continued to provide the right people at the right times in her life.

After more than ten years on the run, Tara is still running. Her family members have spotted her more than once, and she must continually be on guard. But in the midst of all the running, God has provided Tara with a Christian husband.

Most young women cannot imagine paying such a high price to claim Christianity. But this is a story of a real girl in Pakistan who is still running the race with God's help.

Therefore, since we are surrounded by such a great cloud of witnesses, let us throw off everything that hinders and the sin that so easily entangles, and let us run with perseverance the race marked out for us. Let us fix our eyes on Jesus, the author and perfecter of our faith, who for the joy set before him endured the cross, scorning its shame, and sat down at the right hand of the throne of God. Consider him who endured such opposition from sinful men, so that you will not grow weary and lose heart.

(Hebrews 12:1–3)

---

kristen
A LIFE OF SERVICE

People without teeth who drool on themselves should be locked away.

Even though she often thought this, Kristen still took time every week to stop by a care center for old people. She had come to both love and hate the place; she never wanted to go and she felt uncomfortable while there, but she always knew when she left she had done something right. Although she didn't know it then, this feeling would come back to her down the road.

In college, Kristen began to study to be a doctor. Everyone said smart kids went into medicine. No one told her smart kids are also servants. But she found that out the summer she took off and went to the Dominican Republic, an incredibly poor country by the Caribbean Sea. Kristen learned how to cook over open fires, bathe in rivers, jump over open sewers, and collect rainwater to drink. She also learned how to be quiet and still. With no TV, music, or movies, Kristen was forced to face herself and learn more about who and what she was.

One day, the mother of the home where Kristen was staying asked the young woman to braid her hair, which was a tangled, matted mess. Kristen was repulsed by the thought—she had never seen the mother wash her hair. But Kristen gritted her teeth and did the best she could, and when she was done, the mother smiled. It was the first smile Kristen had seen on her face since she had come to share a part of her difficult life. A simple act of kindness had changed her day, and Kristen was reminded that she lived in a world of need, where there were many ways to help and serve every day.

Back at school the next fall, Kristen struggled with premed exams. She studied like crazy and knew the material inside and out, but when it came time to take the tests, she froze. Although she kept trying throughout the year, she began to believe it was God's way of telling her—or her own way of telling herself—that perhaps other plans were on the horizon.

After Kristen graduated, she decided to take a year off to volunteer. Some of her family and friends thought she was crazy. She had given up a career as a doctor and, after four years of college, she was going to work for free? To be honest, it didn't make sense to her either.

That fall, Kristen took a job teaching within the inner city of Chicago. Many of her students were crack babies; 90 percent were on psychotropic meds (medicine used to adjust emotion or behavior), most had extensive criminal records, nearly all were failing school, and all were living in complete poverty. Kristen often cried all the way home after an especially rough day.

Angry teenagers twice Kristen's size called her every name in the book. One student brought a knife to class. When Kristen confronted another for missing class, he said he had been shot in the chest. Then he lifted up his shirt and showed her the actual bullet wounds. Another student threw a computer monitor at the young teacher in frustration. Then one day Kristen was mugged on the train while commuting home.

She couldn't figure it out. She was trying her hardest, but nothing seemed to be going the way she hoped. Had she made a mistake? Was she failing? Was the system failing? Everything seemed too broken; the schools, the kids' lives, even Kristen's faith in God was bruised. There were so many needs, she felt overwhelmed. She wasn't sure she could go on.

But Kristen read the Bible, and there she saw that Jesus taught a lot of wild things, such as in Matthew 5 where He said, "Blessed are the poor in spirit, / for theirs is the kingdom of heaven. / Blessed are those who mourn, / for they will be comforted" (vv. 3–4). As she wrestled with those things, she realized that God designed His children to live in a way that is upside down and inside out. *It's a total 180 compared to every message I get at school or on TV,* Kristen thought. God was confirming that she was headed in the right direction, even when it didn't feel right.

Contrary to all Kristen had learned in college, she suddenly saw that life wasn't about getting. It was about giving. And through giving, she then began to receive. When Kristen released control and gave up what she wanted, she received peace and fulfillment—even in the midst of unending need and outward failure. Kristen found true joy in being who God created her to be. She grew even more convinced that there was something right in serving, even in the midst of things that were so wrong.

This life-changing realization set her free to be more effective and to serve from a full heart. She started by buying a toaster and some bread. Rather than trying to make others fit her agenda, she saw it was time to meet her kids where they were: hungry for both food and love. So she had warm toast ready for them when they showed up for class, and she soon discovered that it was more important to give a kid a high five than it was to teach him how to count to five.

With one young boy named Darrius, Kristen found a mutual language in music. He completed math worksheets in exchange for the chance to watch a music video. He and Kristen practiced reading by looking up lyrics to his favorite songs, printing them out, and sounding out the words. They honed math skills by calculating how many royalties his favorite artist earned every time the radio played his songs. For his birthday, Kristen and Darrius made a collage of, in his words, "the phattest rappers."

Larry, one of Kristen's thirteen-year-old students, could barely read. Over the course of the year, she noticed the slightest changes: a few more words recognized without having to sound them out, fewer incomplete worksheets, many more smiles, and a lot more self-esteem. She really knew, though, that things were on the right track when Larry recognized a need in another student and offered to help.

Someone had once told Kristen, "Your life's work is where the needs of the world and the joys of your heart intersect." She has found that kids are her joy, and their needs are calling out from every corner of the globe. The servant's life is a process; it doesn't come in neat packages. She's faced defeat and discouragement, but she's found that she always has more to give because God fills her again in such amazing ways. Kristen knows she is called to be His hands and serve, one piece of toast at a time.

Whoever wishes to become great among you shall be your servant . . . just as the Son of Man did not come to be served, but to serve, and to give His life a ransom for many.

(Matthew 20:26, 28 NASB)

clare of assisi
FREE FROM THE LOVE OF THE WORLD

C lare Offreduccio was the eldest daughter of a wealthy Italian count living in the tiny town of Assisi near the dawn of the thirteenth century. Her family owned a large palace in Assisi and maintained a castle on the slope of nearby Mount Subasio. Clare's mother was a noblewoman known for her piety and love of the church, and tradition teaches that Clare followed her mother's godly example from a very young age.

Clare was barely eighteen when she heard, perhaps not for the first time, the teaching of another young Assisian named Francis Bernardone. Drawing from traditions established a few centuries earlier by Saint Jerome of Egypt, Saint Augustine of Hippo, and Saint Benedict of Umbria, Francis denounced his family's wealth and adopted a monk's life of poverty. Putting his carefree days as a singer, merchant, and soldier aside, he one day stripped himself naked in the city square, leaving his robes behind as a symbol of the determination with which he was bound to follow Jesus Christ. "I desire no other wealth," he said, "than the poverty of Christ."

Francis's aim was to become a friend of the poor and a lover of the unlovely. He spent many of his days living in caves and shelters and a nearby Benedictine monastery. Other young men followed him into the "Brothers Minor," and they served God together. Francis's work was restoring churches fallen into disrepair and begging alms for the poor and for himself.

When Clare heard Francis give the Lenten service at the church of San Giorgio at Assisi, her heart was struck. She was soon to be married to a man her father selected, but the world had never held much allure for her. She wanted to follow Christ as Francis did. His words inspired her to believe that she, too, could separate herself from the world and live for the sake of God and others.

Accompanied by her aunt, Clare sought out Francis and asked that she be admitted to the way of the Brothers Minor. There was no legal hindrance to her admission, but Francis had made no provision for the inclusion of women into his order. Still, he urged her to pray and be certain of God's calling. She did, and her mind and heart were not changed. She asked again to follow him in the way of service, and touched by her sincerity and convinced of her calling, he agreed.

On Palm Sunday, Clare attended mass in all her finery. As others pressed forward at the altar rail to receive a palm branch from the bishop, Clare remained in her place. That was the last time the world beheld Clare Offreduccio.

She left her father's house that same night, and accompanied by her aunt, she traveled to the chapel of the Portiuncula. The Brothers Minor were there, with candles lit, waiting with Francis to celebrate the mass. After their final amen, Francis read to Clare the laws she would follow. She bowed her head before him in a sign of obedience, and he cut off her hair and left it on the altar. She relinquished her rich robes and received a gray gown and black veil for beginning her life of poverty, chastity, and service. Francis then led Clare away to the convent at San Paolo, where she would live with the Benedictine sisters until a permanent home for her could be secured.

For eighteen years she had been her father's daughter. Now she belonged entirely to God.

The next day, her father learned of her whereabouts and arrived to take her home. He spoke passionately to dissuade her from her promise, but she would not be moved. He finally left her there. A week later, her younger sister Agnes fled from their unhappy home to join Clare, and Francis received her as well. Again their father followed, but his attempts to carry his daughters back home were unsuccessful.

Realizing that he could not keep the sisters safe, Francis moved them to a quiet nearby retreat called San Damiano, which he had rebuilt with his own hands. There they were protected, and San Damiano became the permanent home for the Poor Sisters of Penitence, or "Poor Clares," as they came to be known.

Other noble ladies of Assisi joined them, including, after a time, Clare's third sister, Beatrice, her aunt Pacifica, and even her mother. In this way, the second order of Saint Francis of Assisi was established.

The Poor Clares were not required to travel, preaching and calling men to repentance, or to beg door to door as the Franciscans did. Their duties were fitting to their roles as women and complementary to those of Francis and his followers. They tended the sick, fed the hungry, and made garments for the naked. They fashioned medicines and administered them, made altar cloths for the churches restored by their Franciscan brothers, grew gardens, and baked bread.

Although even the church pressed Clare to renounce her strict vows of poverty, she did not. She meant to own nothing, and own nothing she did. When Cardinal Ugolino (later Pope Gregory IX) visited Clare in Assisi, he urged her to accept provision from Rome for the future needs of the order and offered to absolve her of her previous vows. She steadfastly refused. "Holy Father," she answered, "I crave for absolution from my sin, but I desire not to be absolved from the obligation of following Jesus Christ." Her words earned his lifelong respect.

Saint Clare continued to preside as abbess over the Poor Clares until her death in 1253, nearly forty years after she took her vows. Throughout her life she encouraged and aided her friend and spiritual mentor, Francis. On his final visit to San Damiano, Clare erected a little hut for him in an olive grove close to the monastery. It is believed to be there that he composed his glorious "Canticle of the Sun." Upon Francis's death, the funeral procession carrying his remains stopped only once: at the gate of San Damiano so Clare and her sisters could pay tribute to the one who had challenged them to a life of loving sacrifice for the glory of God.

Live a life worthy of the calling you have received. Be completely humble and gentle; be patient, bearing with one another in love. Make every effort to keep the unity of the Spirit through the bond of peace.

(Ephesians 4:1–3)

jessica klapper
STANDING TALL

Jessica started praying for others when she was five. "I saw answers to my prayers even then," she said. "I knew Jesus was real." She credits her intimate relationship with Jesus Christ to her parents—Christians who have raised her well and loved her through many trials.

At twelve, she spent time with another family, friends of her parents. Nothing unusual happened on the visit, but a few months later, Jessica couldn't get one of the family's sons—Ian—out of her mind.

"At first I dismissed it, wondering briefly how he was doing." Still, Ian kept coming to her mind. She decided to pray for him—every day for several months. "I prayed hard for him. I didn't know what I was praying for specifically, but I kept it up nonetheless." When her family was invited to Ian's home, Jessica told her mother, "Ian's been on my mind. I need to see him and make sure he's all right."

Ian looked fine. Jessica was too embarrassed to ask him how he was doing. She didn't tell him she was praying for him. But her mom told Ian's mom about Jessica's insistent and consistent prayers.

Ian's mom was amazed. "He was very depressed, but we didn't know," she said. "I found him one afternoon in his room, his wrists slit. Since that time, he's made a full recovery." Ian's mom was convinced that Jessica's prayers saved Ian's life.

"What a privilege it was to help Ian in such a time of need. God does hear prayers!" Jessica said.

Jessica spent time doing typical teenage stuff: swimming, scrapbooking, playing laser tag, going to movies. When Jessica was a senior in high school, she was elected president of the Bible club at her high school in South Carolina. She wanted the other thousand members of her school to know about the club's meetings, so she wrote a few sentences to be announced during the daily bulletin. The next day, she waited for the announcement—but it never came. When she asked the receptionist about the omission, she was told to visit the principal.

She sat down in his office, fidgeting. Finally, he spoke. "Announcing a Bible club meeting is a violation of separation of church and state," he said matter-of-factly.

"I don't have any intention of preaching over the PA," Jessica told him. "I just want to inform students about the location and time of a meeting."

The principal denied her request.

Jessica researched the issue and was energized by what she read. "I found documentation saying it was legally acceptable for students to lead and publicize religious-based organizations and events on campus." She presented all her research to her principal, but he again refused to allow the announcement.

Undaunted, Jessica called a law organization known for defending students in similar situations. The lawyers drew up papers—a lawsuit against the district. They sent a copy to

Jessica, the principal, and the attorney for the school district. At that point, Jessica worried. "I got scared and doubted my motivations. Why was it that important to me anyway? Why make waves? I thought and prayed a lot about it, especially after the papers had been served. My intention was to assure the principal that he would be legally covered if he allowed the Bible club announcements."

In the midst of her prayers, she felt God's peace and favor. "I wanted to create a legacy for future Bible clubs—that others could use the PA system, even after I graduated. I wanted to stand up for Jesus."

Jessica waited. And waited. And waited until the last day a response to the lawsuit was required before all the parties involved would have to go to court. On that day, the principal called Jessica down to his office. He had softened and seemed humble. "You have access to the PA system," he said. "And," he added, "you can use any other venue to advertise your group."

Jessica thanked him and immediately made her announcement over the PA system to the entire school. She hung posters and handed out fliers. She even set up a table in the lunchroom that advertised information about the True Love Waits campaign (a national group that advocates sexual abstinence).

"I didn't say much to anyone about what had transpired the previous weeks," she says. "But I made sure I told people about what a privilege it is to have the freedom to advertise Bible-based religious events."

Still, Jessica fretted about how her actions had affected her principal. "I worried a lot about what the principal thought of me, so I prayed. My prayers were answered when the faculty voted for me to receive the only available scholarship for graduates that year," she said. "My principal handed me the award on stage and smiled warmly. I could tell that he approved of me and wasn't angry."

Jessica has continued to learn to stand tall. She failed to listen to her parents about a guy she was dating—someone who ended up abusing her. Although the experience was excruciating, she saw God's protection shielding her. Now she shares her experience openly with others. "I have been able to talk to other young ladies about the dangers of abusive boyfriends," she says, "and how to recover after a relationship."

Jessica also has had to learn how to assert herself in medical situations because she is plagued by unremitting seizures and ill health. "I went to doctor after doctor with no answers— dead ends," she says, "but it led me to study medicine." While in nursing school, she was able to diagnose herself with hypoglycemia—something no doctor could earlier pinpoint. She is managing her health now.

Jessica prayed through another painful time when her fiancé left. "His life was on a downward spiral. I was spared from a lot of trouble and heartache," she notes today. Simultaneously, Jessica's mom was hospitalized. So Jessica helped homeschool her younger brother Jacob while attending college full-time. "God really showed His mercy to me during that time," she says.

Whether praying for a suicidal acquaintance, standing up for religious freedom in school, or walking through the pitfalls of life, Jessica has seen God meet her in every way—a miracle that keeps her grounded in her faith. And she is gaining the respect of her friends and community.

"To this day," Jessica says, "I believe if you pray and stand up for Jesus, others will respect you."

I am not ashamed of the gospel, because it is the power of God for the salvation of everyone who believes: first for the Jew, then for the Gentile.

(Romans 1:16)

WEEK TWO JOURNAL

—◆·◆—

⊨ Do you feel God is "messing up" somewhere in the world?

⊨ What would it take for you to begin to trust Him, regardless of the outcome?

⊨ Do you feel as if you are too much of a "mess" yourself for God to use you in a messed-up world?

⊨ If you could pick a way to be part of His plan, how would you like God to use you?

⊨ What Bible verse or passage of Scripture has been most meaningful to you this week? Why?

norah ashkar
FAITH AND FILM

"No offense," said a fellow New York University student to aspiring filmmaker Norah Ashkar, "but I hate Jesus." Norah had never even said His name. Her class had just finished viewing her first black-and-white short film, and during the ensuing critique one of her classmates quickly took issue with the visual references it contained to her Christian faith. The images were subtle ones—a loaf of bread on a kitchen counter and a nearby box of Life cereal paying silent tribute to the "bread of life"—but they were not overlooked. Her sharp-eyed critic loudly and passionately voiced his disapproval, and soon he was not alone.

While she admits his outburst stung, Norah says she wasn't particularly surprised by the reaction her piece generated. Her early semesters in the creative community at New York University film school had taught her that tolerance is a widely praised but selectively practiced virtue. "The other students here are tolerant if they like you," she explains, "but if you don't fit in, they don't like you very much. They all believe the same basic stuff, and they expect you to believe it too. If you don't, you're the odd man out."

First drawn to animation as a career, Norah began exercising her creative gifts early. A self-proclaimed doodler, during high school she attended a summer program in animation at the University of Southern California and followed it the next summer with one at NYU, where she admittedly caught the film bug. Then she applied for entrance to both universities and began to pray—not simply that she'd be accepted at one or the other, but that she would be allowed to attend either one.

One of twin daughters in a tightly knit family, Norah comes from a mixed home: her mother is a Christian and her father a Muslim. He did not favor his daughters attending out-of-state schools and was not at all receptive to their growing faith. "We didn't talk about it," she says, "ever. We used to say when we were going to church that we were going to hang out with friends. I'm sure he knew *where* we were meeting those friends, but we didn't flaunt it, so he didn't ask."

When the hoped-for acceptance letter arrived from NYU, Norah asked her friends to pray and sat down with her father to discuss her future. To her utter delight and relief, their prayers were answered. He allowed his daughter to move to New York City, and a new adventure of faith began.

Although she tried to prepare for what she felt would be a lack of spiritual support in her newly adopted city by e-mailing churches in Manhattan and putting out feelers for connections with other believers, Norah acknowledges that it was difficult at first to establish a network of friends. She laughingly remembers what she calls "the day I met my first Christian at school—a volleyball player from San Diego in a Switchfoot T-shirt." Seeing the shirt promoting a Christian band, she approached him and asked about his faith. When he said he was a Christian, she quickly replied, "Me too" and recalls that he seemed as relieved to find her as she was to find him.

Slowly, Norah began to piece together a web of like-minded fellow artists, both within the university and outside it. "I attended a Campus Crusade winter conference," she says. "That helped me connect with some other folks I might not have otherwise met, and things just sort of grew from there."

Soon Norah became a regular at transFORM, a monthly meeting in Manhattan where Christian artists gather, both to interpret popular culture and to show one another their work. Along the way she also met established believing artists such as New Yorker Makoto Fujimura, founder of the International Arts Movement (IAM) and a presidential appointee to the National Council on the Arts. These interactions with artists of deep faith and strong influence had a profound impact on Norah and offered plenty of life-giving encouragement.

Her continued association with peers in the art world has taught Norah that excellence in her craft can give her a hearing where her faith alone would likely prevent her being heard. "They think they've heard the truth. They think they know it. But many of us who believe are talented too. We're good artists, and in this environment, talent is respected."

In her classes at NYU, Norah's goal is to show up, work hard, get assignments in on time, and be supportive of her fellow students. Her work ethic and positive attitude have already found favor with some of her toughest professors—including ones whose beliefs are strongly opposed to her own. She's found a mentor too—an NYU instructor who has observed her diligence and believes in her talent. That association led to her first paying job as an artist—a summer internship as an office/production assistant on an MGM film featuring Steve Martin as the Pink Panther. It was Norah's first film industry paycheck, and she was pleased to have had the opportunity to earn it.

Norah will finish her studies soon and wonders what the future will hold. She's chosen an industry that she admits is not at all sympathetic to her beliefs, and she knows the way will not be easy. "But this is the dream God has given me," she affirms, "and I'm going to follow it."

She offers this advice for other aspiring artists who might come after her: "Work hard. Don't be afraid to go for your dream. Find a group of friends whose support you can count on, and be an encourager for them too. Most of all, trust God, and put your focus on following Him." She says, "I learned this verse a long time ago, and I'm finding out every day how true it really is: 'Greater is He who is in you than he who is in the world' [1 John 4:4 NASB]."

Norah not only believes it—she's counting on it to sustain her in a world that hates the One she loves.

You, dear children, are from God and have overcome them, because the one who is in you is greater than the one who is in the world.

(1 John 4:4)

---

breṭṭ ṭrapolino

GOD'S OPEN DOOR

The assignment: move with your husband of eight years and your three young children to a place you've never seen. Adjust to the unfamiliar rhythms and practices of a Third World country, and learn a language completely unknown to you. Live at first with a young pastor, his wife, and *their* small children in a home barely big enough for them. And for an added challenge, prepare for the birth of your fourth child in a place where modern medical facilities are severely limited and infant mortality is high.

This is not a nightmare. Instead, it's the very scenario that causes Brett Trapolino's eyes to sparkle with joy, and the corners of her mouth to turn up in a shy but easy smile. She confesses that while she is unsure about what God might have in store for her, she's thrilled at the prospect of following Him into the unknown.

When Kirby and Brett Trapolino married, neither had any idea that they might one day live in Ongole, India, partnering with local believers to support and serve an orphanage, a Bible college, and a church-planting ministry. Kirby met Pastor

B. Samson, head of what is now Peace Gospel Ministries, when he was single, and Samson was the twenty-year-old son of a beggar, preaching in the slums of Southern India. But the two men formed a bond that would change both their lives.

"Kirby helped me by raising funds in the United States," says Samson. "He encouraged me to press on in the Lord, to dream big, and to believe that the Lord could do it, even though I was living on three dollars a week as a slum pastor."

Kirby continued to support Samson's work and to visit India, even after he and Brett married and began their family. In the States, the young couple launched a business together, moved to the suburbs, and began to serve in their local church. But over time, the land and people that had captured Kirby's heart nearly a decade before began to call Brett too.

And the time seemed right to go. Peace Gospel was supporting thirty orphans in three temporary shelters and had trained seventy-six full-time ministers and planted forty-two churches in remote villages. Bible studies were being translated into the Telugu language for the first time. The Trapolinos' treasure had been invested in India, and their hearts were ready to follow it there.

"Even while we live in the here and now," says Brett, "God is always preparing us for the next thing. What we're living now—this is not it. God wants to give us other comforts. He wants us to know mystery, to trust Him, and to wonder. I'm hungry to fulfill what He has made me to do, and He's redefining what greatness looks like to me."

Having grown up Catholic, Brett says she had known about God since she was a child. But it was in college that her faith in Christ became real to her, although she readily admits that she struggled with an eating disorder and with periodic bouts of depression. A theater major, Brett remembers participating in a guided exercise in one acting class that became a personal turning point in her life. "Someone is waiting for you," the instructor said. And as Brett moved toward that "waiting one" in her imagination, she says simply, "It was Jesus. And I knew that it was Him."

When she reflects on her journey so far, Brett says, "God has shown me so much mercy. When He has a purpose for someone's life, it will not be thwarted. He's given me many second chances. I probably shouldn't even be alive, and I'm the mother of three, expecting another baby and facing a huge change in life without the kind of fear I might have once had. But I believe that what the Bible says in 1 John is true: 'Perfect love casts out fear' [4:18 NASB]. This season for me is about hearing Him in the small things—about learning to serve, to stay hidden, and to esteem others more than myself. I love what He is teaching me. And I want to know Him more."

Although the move to India was well under way when Brett learned she was expecting, the pregnancy did not change the Trapolinos' plans. "We did pray about it," Brett says, "but Kirby and I both believed we were still to go, even though in the world's eyes, it seemed foolish. We knew that God had opened the door and that there was no other way for us but to go through it."

As a result of the pregnancy, Brett couldn't get any of the immunizations recommended for the family before they left the country. And the physician who delivered her first three children issued strong warnings about the prenatal care (or lack of it) she could expect to receive in India.

On her final visit to that physician, Brett prayed that God would speak a blessing over her through her unbelieving doctor, and He did. "She made it clear she was against my going," says Brett. "And she told me all the things that might go wrong. I didn't argue with her. I thanked her. But I also told her as gently as I could that I knew God had given us this baby at this time, and that He could care for it even in such difficult circumstances."

Then, Brett told her very professional, capable, and matter-of-fact physician that she loved and respected her and strongly desired to have her blessing on both her pregnancy and her plans to have the baby in India. And the same doctor who had never demonstrated any overt affection to her patient stood, embraced Brett warmly, and gave her that blessing.

For Brett, it was a very physical reminder of what God continues to do in the lives of those He loves: "God doesn't run out of blessings. He has a dream for each and every man and woman. Our job is to delight in who He has made us to be—to walk with Him and to rejoice in that. My prayer each day is that God would let us know more and more what it is to fall in love with Jesus—and give us the courage and desire to follow Him anywhere."

I can do everything through him who gives me strength.

(Philippians 4:13)

katherine von bora
CALLED TO BE DIFFERENT

Tiny Katherine von Bora was only five years old when her father left her at the gates of the Benedictine convent school near Brehna, Germany. Katherine's mother had died that same year, and her father soon remarried. A small daughter was too much of a burden, and her father felt that in the convent she would at least receive a good education. Once there, her options were few. So, although Katherine never aspired to the secluded life of a nun, five years later she was transferred to a convent in nearby Nimbschen and made her vows when she was only sixteen years old.

Even though she hadn't planned for a life of seclusion, poverty, and chastity, Katherine submitted herself to the rigorous routine of sixteenth-century life in the convent. She received the education of a teacher, learning some Latin at a time when many women could not even read in their native tongue. She learned to cook and garden and sew. She said her prayers and attended church services each day.

When Katherine was in her early twenties, the preaching of a man named Martin Luther began to penetrate the convent walls. Luther was a former monk himself and had left the monastery when he came to believe through his personal study of God's Word that men were saved by faith through grace alone, and not by works of penance or good deeds or service to the church. His preaching in sixteenth-century Germany was causing quite a stir. The German church was still under the authority of the Roman Catholic pope, and Luther's words stirred not only those within the church, but the common men and women of Germany as well.

When Katherine and her friends began to consider his words, they appealed to Luther for help in leaving the convent. Many had not come to the service of the church under their own free will and felt it was holding them prisoner. Luther even wrote a letter to several nuns about their plight: "Dear sisters . . . You are correct that there are two reasons for which life at the convent and vows may be forsaken: The one is where men's laws and life within the order are being forced, where there is no free choice, where it is put upon the conscience as a burden. In such cases it is time to run away, leaving the convent and all it entails behind."[1]

So, on Easter eve in 1523, Katherine and eleven other nuns escaped from the convent at Nimbschen, hidden in the wagon of a merchant named Leonard Koppe. Three of the nuns were returned to the homes of their families. The other nine were taken to Wittenburg, where Luther himself hoped to find them all homes, husbands, or positions of some sort. In the end, all were provided for but one. Her name was Katherine von Bora.

Two years after her escape, Katherine was living still with a family in Wittenburg as a domestic servant. She had fallen in love with a young man who promised to marry her, but his parents objected to her status as a former nun. She was brokenhearted. Luther proposed another arranged marriage for her, but she refused the man he suggested. She wasn't trying to be difficult, although Luther may have thought so. He found her somewhat arrogant when in fact she was embarrassed by her awkward position.

Still, when a friend of Luther's came to visit, she hinted to him that Luther might be an acceptable husband to her—partly because it seemed so unlikely, and Luther's age (almost sixteen years her senior) suggested he might never marry.

When Luther heard her words, he did not take Katherine's suggestion seriously but spoke of it to his parents when he went home to visit. Instead of laughing about it, his father seized upon the idea. His son was not getting any younger, and the elder Luther hinted that he might like to have some grandchildren!

What started as a kind of jest became more and more attractive to Luther. By marrying Katherine, he could give her the status she needed, give testimony to his own faith, spite the pope, and give his father comfort in his old age.

So the former monk, Luther, took as his wife the former nun, Katherine, on the thirteenth of June 1525. To Leonard Koppe, the man who smuggled his wife-to-be out of the convent, Luther wrote this letter of invitation: "I am going to get married. God likes to work miracles and to make a fool of the world. You must come to the wedding." He did.

Some serve God by remaining single for life. Others serve God by marrying. Martin and Katherine made a life together that impacted many lives for God. They moved into a run-down Augustinian cloister in Wittenburg, which Katherine made into a home. Luther never cared for money and did not manage it well. Katherine did, and she kept their household supplied and her husband fortified. They had six children and took in several nieces and nephews. Students at the nearby university boarded with them, and there were often thirty or more people living together under their roof.

Katherine ably ran their home, and Luther preached, wrote, and taught the Bible at the university and in the church. Luther spoke of his wife often and with great affection; he called her "my rib" and just as often "my lord Katie." With Katherine, Luther saw marriage as a school for character, saying that he learned more about grace from it than from all his studies, books, and sermons. He paid her perhaps the highest tribute when he called Paul's letter to the Galatians about freedom "my Katherine von Bora."

Theirs may not have been a love match from the beginning, but their love grew. What began as fondness and gratitude for companionship increased greatly through the years, and Martin and Katherine's marriage became the pattern for couples in ministry together for hundreds of years hence. Without Katherine's love and strong support, Luther could not have served God as effectively as he did. And without Luther's belief in and love for his wife, Katherine's life would have been a shadow of what it was. "Katie," he told her, "you have married an honest man who loves you; you are an empress."

Both of them regarded their marriage as a vocation as serious and glorious and binding as their vows to the church had once been. Luther would change the church forever; but it was Katherine von Bora who made the biggest change in Luther.

Trust in the LORD with all your heart
and lean not on your own understanding;
in all your ways acknowledge him,
and he will make your paths straight.

(Proverbs 3:5–6)

katlyn mcgee
LEARNING TO TRUST GOD

"You have a brain tumor in your right temporal lobe," the doctor told twenty-two-year-old Katlyn McGee. As the news settled into her heart and the shock permeated her soul, Katlyn recounted God's faithfulness to her.

Growing up in a Christian home, Katlyn had given her life to Jesus when she was seven years old and was soon baptized alongside her mother. As a child, Katlyn understood she was a sinner in need of God's forgiveness and grace.

On the day she met Jesus, her parents rejoiced. "They were so happy to know that I would be with them one day in heaven, that I had found my best friend," she relates.

But something happened when Katlyn hit adolescence. During her sophomore and junior years of high school, she straddled two worlds—her church world, where she played the part of youth-group member and said all the right things, and her friend world, where she delved into secret sin.

"While everyone else thought my life was great, inside I was falling apart," she remembers. "During this time, because of my rebellion, I felt so distant from the Lord. Instead of feeling His presence in my life, I felt hopeless, depressed, and empty and wondered if I even had a purpose in life. Some days, I wished I wasn't alive.

"I walked in sin, hoping that the lifestyle would bring me friends, happiness, acceptance, and love. Yet I never did fit in. Instead I ended up by myself a lot, discouraged, ready to give up on life."

As the doctor's stark office reeled around her, Katlyn remembered the summer that changed her life. During the summer of 1998, prior to her senior year of high school, she attended Super Summer, a Christian leadership camp. There, God exposed her rebellious heart. She told God she was sorry for all the pain she'd caused Him, her family, her friends. He met her with forgiveness and healing for the wounds from her two years of rebellion.

"As a seventeen-year-old," she says, "I came to a place of total surrender to Christ in every area of my life. I gave Him my past, my present, and my future. I knew the Lord intimately for the first time. Looking back, I don't even remember the girl I used to be because He's changed my life so much."

During her senior year, Katlyn changed from a public school to Trinity Christian High School. "It was there the Lord began to restore 'the years the locusts have eaten' [Joel 2:25]. I found hope through the Lord, deep friendships, and strong mentoring relationships."

After only a few months at Trinity, her class voted her homecoming queen, something Katlyn attributes to God's faithfulness to renew her life. "I was not the most popular girl, but I got to know everyone in my school, accepting people for who they were."

Because Katlyn longed to be a missionary, she took a year off after high school to explore mission work. Her first trip took her to India. "I saw lame, crippled, deformed people everywhere, but I found so much joy serving the Lord in India. When a street kid said good-bye and that he'd see me in heaven someday, I realized going out on a limb, trusting God to do with my life what He wills, was so much better than standing on a comfortable foundation of self-sufficiency and independence."

Katlyn enrolled in Texas Tech University in Lubbock, Texas, after her year off. While there, she became a student intern at Bacon Heights Baptist Church, leading junior-high, high-school, and college students. It was during that time of college and ministry that she started having bouts of memory loss. Her moods swung violently on an uncontrolled axis. A few times, she blacked out. When she came to, she didn't know where she was or what she was doing.

Initially, she thought the stress of college life at Texas Tech was taking its toll, but as her symptoms persisted and medication had little effect, she decided to see a specialist.

"Youth is a time of infinite days, hours, and minutes to be spent enjoying carefree life," she notes. "However, in October of 2003 my ideas about youth and life were radically changed." When she told her friends about the tumor, it was as if she were talking about someone else, something else. Her shocked family members couldn't wrap their minds and hearts around the fact that Katlyn had a large tumor pressing on her brain.

Katlyn worried about many things. Would she die? Would she lose her memory for good? Would there be complications?

Ten days after the initial diagnosis, Katlyn was wheeled into the operating room. "I was overwhelmed, scared," she says. "There, alone on the operating table, it was just the Lord and me. I felt His overwhelming presence right before surgery. He gave me peace. I knew that should I die, it would still be to His glory. In that moment, I was not afraid. Through it all, my family and I trusted the Lord and were able to say, 'Blessed be Your name no matter what the circumstance.'"

The surgeons successfully removed the atypical tumor. They sent the tissues to several labs across the country while Katlyn and her family awaited the prognosis. One month later, Johns Hopkins called and said the tumor was benign—no further treatment required.

Katlyn learned much through her health crisis, particularly about God's goodness during difficult situations. "I would go through the bad times again to know the Lord the way I do now and to be able to look back in awe and amazement at where He's brought me, what He's done in my life, and how He's allowed me to be used by Him for His glory."

She has a desire to honor God regardless of what life hands her. "I want to be like Job when trials come," she says. "Instead of complaining, cursing God, and giving up on faith, I want to fall to the ground, worship, and love Him—no matter what comes my way."

Katlyn McGee still remembers her life in snapshots of God's faithfulness. "I daily feel my scar to remind me of the Lord's faithfulness," she says. "I touch it to remember one of the best days of my life, lying on the operating table, feeling the Lord so near."

God demonstrates his own love for us in this: While we were still sinners, Christ died for us.

(Romans 5:8)

Megan
GOD IS SOVEREIGN

Megan had done short-term missions before and loved each one, and the next trip promised to be even bigger and better than the rest. Her group's destination was exotic, and the needs of the people were immeasurable. Megan expected to come home stronger, triumphant, and more energized in her faith. But God had other things in mind. . . .

On the flight back to the United States, while others slept to the steady hum of the engines, Megan tried to catch up on some journaling. The mission itself had been even more amazing than she'd expected. The street ministry, the leper colony, the cultural exposure, the tight relationships on the team—she couldn't have asked for more.

But as she wrote, something began to stir inside her. Images began to flash in her mind. Megan couldn't shake them from her thoughts. Shoving aside all the other memories, she kept seeing the loving but pain-filled eyes of a woman named Shanta.

In Shanta's country, it's not uncommon for fathers or husbands to sell their daughters or wives for brutal lives of prostitution in a neighboring country. Since HIV is common in that region, it doesn't take long for the virus to infiltrate the girls' bodies. As soon as the symptoms of AIDS begin to show, the girls are thrown out on the streets, where the horrors of forced prostitution are replaced by the reality of total abandonment. The alleys and the garbage dumps become their homes and kitchens while they await long, drawn-out deaths.

Day after day, Shanta goes out to find these starving and sick young women. She takes them to her home, where she loves them as her own daughters and shares with them the love and message of Jesus. Some she is able to nurse back to health. But most she comforts as best she can while AIDS takes what remains of their lives. In the midst of all the pain and poverty, Shanta's home is a safe haven to the few girls fortunate enough to live there.

Megan had been in Shanta's home for only a couple of hours. But as the memories of her and the girls replayed in her mind, the framework of her life as she knew it began to crumble.

Back home in the U.S., everything was the same as Megan had left it, yet everything seemed different. At school she tried to be normal—pretending that she was listening in class, that she cared about her grades, that it mattered about who was dating whom—but she couldn't get her emotions under control. Megan found her heart riddled with anger, guilt, depression, and judgment. She tried to get back into a comfortable groove, but she just couldn't make her pre-mission life work anymore. Nothing seemed to fit.

Worse, she couldn't get God to fit anymore. Megan couldn't find Him in her new view of a cruel and uncertain world. Something had to change. Megan had to do something. Restless and anxious, she decided to take action. Surrounded by the darkness of the night, she turned on her computer and began typing.

Dear Friends and Family in Christ,

This summer God blessed me with the opportunity to serve Him in a small Hindu country at the foot of Mt. Everest. . . . Here women and girls, many around the ages of six or seven, are sold into prostitution where they are used 24 hours a day, 7 days a week, until their bodies are worn out. . . . It is 4:30 in the morning here as I write this letter. I sleep warm and safe in my bed and down the hall I have two parents who love me. But it is 4:30 in the afternoon there, and girls are living lives that would only appear in my very worst nightmares.

She then explained about the refuge and healing Shanta provides.

Please pray for Shanta, that she will be filled with encouragement. Pray for her finances. Pray for the thousands of girls who don't make it to Shanta's home. Would you pray too that they will find out about Jesus, so they won't have to die alone? . . . If you feel God calling you to give financially to support Shanta's work, please let me know.

Megan sent the letter to fifteen close friends and family members, and several sent money. Encouraged, she sent out a few more letters and more money began to arrive. A short while later, Megan was asked to speak at her church and then other churches, and then at business clubs. People continued to give. The newspaper featured a story, and donations started coming through the mail.

After Megan had gathered about twenty-two thousand dollars, she quit counting! With the money, Shanta bought a little bit of land and began to build a "rescue station" on the border where she and her staff could intercept young girls on their way to the prostitution trade. Shanta used some of the money to buy back freedom. Some paid for the comfort of the dying, and other dollars made it possible to train women to be self-supporting.

This should have been enough to quiet Megan's soul, but inside, she raged against the evil that continued in Shanta's country. Dozens were being rescued, but thousands of girls were still being lost. How could God look into the eyes of one little girl and save her while ignoring the pleading eyes of another taken prisoner?

One day Megan took a hike alone, walking without direction or destination, stumbling in the snow. She felt small and alone. Girls were being saved as a result of her taking action, but what about those who were still being swept away? Why didn't God do something?

Megan wept and shouted. She told God everything. Then she curled up in the snow, exhausted, and in the quiet she began to heal. Slowly, with certainty, a peace in the midst of not understanding began to seep into her heart: *Do I see better than He does?* she questioned. *Do I think I could do better than God? He is ultimately good. He knows, and He cares. Who am I to question the way He moves or doesn't? He is God, I am not. If I will trust Him, I will find rest.*

That day Megan retraced her steps in the snow, and eventually she retraced her steps all the way back to Shanta's home, spending a month in her country with her girls, her pain, and her spark of hope in such dark places.

When she left, she knew that what God wanted to accomplish in and through her was complete. She could move on. During the flight back, there was again much to think about, much Megan had learned from Shanta and her country:

~ Someday she would see things clearly and understand, but not fully on this side of the grave.
~ She needed to be a woman of action, regardless of whether or not she understood God's work in the situation.
~ Her walk with God was based on faith in His goodness, not her feelings or her perceptions of evil around her.
~ Someday, it wouldn't be like this. God has promised a better world.

Someday this will be true, and Megan chooses by faith to believe it. Someday there will be peace and warmth, even for little girls living in the cold shadows of Mount Everest.

He will wipe every tear from their eyes. There will be no more death or mourning or crying or pain, for the old order of things has passed away.

(Revelation 21:4)

WEEK THREE JOURNAL

—◆◆—

⇢ What are some of your greatest fears?

⇢ If you could be certain God is with you no matter what, how would it affect your worries?

⇢ If you were free from your fears, in what new ways would you be able to love and serve others?

⇢ How would being free from fear affect your worship and your prayers?

⇢ What Bible verse or passage of Scripture has been most meaningful to you this week? Why?

Mulahn

FOLLOWER OF CHRIST

Like a crudely fashioned bracelet, Mulahn's wrist is encircled in marred flesh—a result of torture at the hands of Muslim kidnappers. Captors singed her skin with sulfuric acid, erasing the carefully tattooed cross there. The cross had been Mulahn's quiet proclamation that she was a Christian amid a culture of Islam. Somehow, Egyptian captors determined to sear Christ from her heart by burning her skin.

Mulahn grew up in Egypt in a Christian home. Her family represented a small religious minority in Egypt—the Coptic Christians numbering six million. Islamic fundamentalists began targeting Coptics in the 1990s, believing them to be a real threat to Islam.

These Islamic zealots roamed the streets, looking for Coptics to harass and abduct. Mulahn's closely woven community lived against that constant backdrop of worry, wondering if that day would bring yet another abduction. They were very cautious about whom they trusted and where they traveled.

On one ordinary day, a group called the Gamat Islamiya abducted eighteen-year-old Mulahn while she was visiting friends. They spirited her away, and her abductors raped her repeatedly. They knew that if they did so, they'd essentially ruin Mulahn's life—if they stole her innocence, they stole her ability in her culture ever to marry.

Everything they did was deliberate. Every torture they invented had a purpose: to dissuade her from Christianity and her culture.

During the ordeal, her captors moved her in stealth, blindfolded and brutalized, to dingy hideouts. They worked day and night to convert her heart and mind to Islam and undermine her connection to Jesus Christ. "Pray to Allah!" they demanded. To survive, Mulahn had to do as they said, bowing low to the ground, facing Mecca.

The kidnappers made Mulahn memorize pages of the Koran. Through sleep and food deprivation, mind-numbing memorization sessions, forced prayer, and repeated rape, Mulahn began to bend to her captors' wishes.

Mulahn's traumatized father sought help from the Cairo police. "You must find her," he told them. "They will torture her." Hot tears erupted from his dark eyes. "You must find her."

"Forget Mulahn," a police officer told him. "She's now safe in the hands of Islam."

"You don't understand. They have *taken* my daughter."

"*You* don't understand!" the officer shot back. "You must sign this now." He shoved a document toward Mulahn's father, handing him a pen. The piece of paper declared that he would not search for his daughter. "Sign it!"

"I cannot sign this."

"If you don't, you will be responsible for any harm that comes her way. If your family searches for her, she will be hurt. Mulahn is safe. She is being retrained in the ways of Islam. If you love her, you will leave her alone. Allah will take care of her."

With shaking hand, Mulahn's father signed the document, his tears blurring his signature. Still, he searched for her in secret, relentless in his pursuit.

During her "retraining," Mulahn's kidnappers required her to wear a veil, the traditional *hijab* Islamic women wear for the sake of modesty. Initially, she refused. "They warned me that if I removed it, they would throw acid on my face," she later recounted. After days upon days of brainwashing torture, she acquiesced to her captors and signed papers saying she was a convert to Islam. She quit fighting the veil.

And then, one day, she escaped.

A clandestine group called Servants of the Cross arranged for her rescue. This group sheltered her, nourished her. It protected her from harm and kept her safe from her captors.

Egyptian *Shari'a* law considers conversion from Islam to Christianity illegal—an offense that carries a swift death sentence. Even so, the Servants helped Mulahn find her way back to Christianity. Instead of demanding she shroud herself in a veil, the Servants gave her light. Instead of depriving her, they gave her food. Instead of forcing her to pray, they prayed for her.

The group helped Mulahn in other ways too. Because Egyptian law places the sole blame upon rape victims, not the rapists, the state often gives the victims a death sentence. Other rape victims are not allowed to marry; they are considered damaged. But the Servants introduced Mulahn to a Christian who later became her husband.

One Servant explained, "I supervise between thirty and thirty-five re-conversions every month. In all Egypt there are between seven thousand and ten thousand cases of forced conversions to Islam. It is our duty to save them."[1]

Reunited with her family, Mulahn is now married and following Jesus Christ. She still lives in fear, and her nightmares are a constant reminder of her nine months of Islamic torture. But she is alive. And she has hope.

With the help of the Servants of the Cross, a tattooist placed another cross on Mulahn's wrist, just above her bracelet of torture. Today, she dares to be a follower of Jesus Christ—in a culture that longs to sear His cross from their land with disfiguring acid.

Blessed is the man who perseveres under trial, because when he has stood the test, he will receive the crown of life that God has promised to those who love him.

(James 1:12)

Marolda

A SEA OF FORGIVENESS

Marolda and her college friends, a group of singers who called themselves One Voice, wanted to do something good for their community around Christmastime. They asked Marolda to look for an organization in need of their time or money. Starting with the phone directory, Marolda began placing calls to local nonprofit agencies. Before long she connected with the warm and enthusiastic director of a crisis pregnancy center. Marolda didn't know it then, but that call would change her life.

Sylvia, the director of the center, invited the girls to come for a visit on a Sunday afternoon. As a result of what they saw, three members of One Voice signed up to train as volunteer counselors—and Marolda was one of them.

The questionnaire for prospective volunteers asked, "Have you ever had an abortion?" The next question read, "If yes, how many abortions have you had?" Just six months before, Marolda had become pregnant. When she told the father of the baby, he offered to pay for an abortion and drove her to the clinic they selected for the procedure. A short time later, she became pregnant again, and that time she chose abortion alone, telling no one.

In a previous conversation with Sylvia, Marolda had admitted to her first abortion. Since Sylvia knew from her work that many young women Marolda's age in the United States have had at least one abortion, she was not surprised. But what the bright, intelligent, hardworking college student saw as an understandable one-time mistake seemed inexcusable when it happened again. Especially twice in the same year.

So she had admitted the second abortion to no one. Not her friends. Not the father of the baby. Not even her mother, who drove her to a private doctor's office for the second abortion, thinking her daughter was having a simple outpatient procedure to correct a medical problem.

Faced with the question in black and white, Marolda hesitated. "I told you I'd had one abortion," she said to Sylvia, "but really I've had two."

"Okay," said the center director. "Put two."

Marolda's history of abortion meant that to volunteer, she needed to go through not only regular volunteer training, but intensive postabortion training as well. She agreed, but she says the experience was not easy. "I was antsy and irritated. It was nine weeks of intense digging through my past—every Tuesday for two long hours."

Raised in Antigua by her Anglican grandparents, Marolda had grown into an intelligent, goal-oriented, self-sufficient young woman who had hoped to become a physician, like several other members of her extended family. She moved to the United States to attend college and enrolled as a biology student. But other circumstances from her past lay just under the surface of her polished, engaging exterior.

She had had virtually no relationship with her father growing up; her mother raised her daughter alone during Marolda's first years, then moved to the States to get her own education and establish herself so that they could eventually be reunited. As a teenager Marolda was raped, but it remained a secret. Although she was raised in church and believed in God, Marolda found her experience with Him changed after her first abortion.

"I was alone, lonely, sad, and bleeding. I called the guy who was the father. He didn't come. I went from my bed to the bathroom and lay down on the floor. Then I did something I'd never done before. I cried out to Jesus. I just cried out His name. And He was there."

Slowly, through postabortion training and the satisfaction of helping young women who found themselves in the same situation she had twice confronted, Marolda felt life seemed to be turning around for her. She met Bryan, the minister of music at a local church, who would later become her husband. Soon the crisis pregnancy center offered her a full-time job as a volunteer coordinator. She accepted, putting her studies on hold.

The world was righting itself. Life was good . . . until Marolda became pregnant a third time. This time, she wasn't a student. She was an employee of a crisis pregnancy center, dating a young minister. Feeling guilty, depressed, and ashamed, Marolda was sure of only one thing: she would not have another abortion. Bryan agreed. And there would be no secrets. They told their respective families, who offered support. Bryan told the leadership of his church. And Marolda told Sylvia. Together, the two of them went before the board of directors of the pregnancy center and told them.

The board suggested she and Bryan marry immediately,

and if they did so, Marolda could keep her job. Although she wanted to marry Bryan, she refused. "I knew I had a sin issue that needed to be dealt with," she says. "I needed to repent, be forgiven, and finish the hard work of healing. I didn't need to hide again—I needed to allow God to complete the work He had begun."

It was one of the lowest points of Marolda's life. She was pregnant, unemployed, unmarried, and disappointed in herself. She and Bryan began to get counseling together. "I told myself, 'What a fool you are,'" says Marolda. "But God is so faithful. He met me right where I was and loved me."

God would have one more unexpected challenge for Marolda. In September of 2002, she and Bryan learned through amniocentesis that their baby might have spina bifida. Doctors recommended an ultrasound to explore further. What the test revealed was a second-trimester baby boy with no abnormalities. They had already decided that whatever they learned would not change their plans to have the baby. But later that day, Bryan asked Marolda if she was ready to marry him, and she said yes.

On February 22, 2003, a thirty-two-week-pregnant Marolda married the father of her son in a celebration that included their closest family and friends. The bride wore the largest bridal gown she could find. Their son was born a few weeks later.

Today the college student who wanted to do something good for a crisis pregnancy center to soothe her conscience is now counseling pregnant women again. Her former boss, Sylvia, opened another center serving the inner city and invited Marolda to come on board as director of client services. "I was a stay-at-home mom, loving life with my husband and our baby, and God said, 'Come out of your cave, Marolda, I'm ready to use you again.'" She also counsels postabortive women, because she knows it is possible to put aside living in guilt and shame.

And Marolda still sings.

For as high as the heavens are above the earth,
so great is his love for those who fear him;
as far as the east is from the west,
so far has he removed our transgressions from us.

(Psalm 103:11–12)

---

amy carmichael

LOVING OTHERS

Amy Carmichael was born to a devout Presbyterian family on December 16, 1867, on the north coast of Ireland. When she was a child, her curiosity was strong, and her favorite playground was the rocky beach where she explored the little things that were alive in the ocean's tide. She loved the adventure she found in the outdoors.

She was not a conventional little girl. Once, given a beautiful dollhouse completely furnished with exquisite furniture and elaborately dressed dolls, she surprised her nanny by emptying out all the furniture and filling the house with moss, stones, and beetles. Amy found those things much more interesting.

Her parents surrounded all their children with beauty. They taught them to be observers and learners, told them exciting stories, gave them many pets to love, and taught them about God's love. Life was full, and Amy was a very happy child.

Even when young, Amy showed a deep sensitivity toward the pain of others. When her mother first told her the story of Jesus' crucifixion, she ran outside to find solace in the garden.

She could not understand how anyone could take the life of a man so special and good.

She later recalled a lesson she had in prayer at age three. She knew God answered prayer and so knelt by her bed one night, asking for blue eyes, quite confident that she would have them in the morning. At dawn, she jumped out of bed to check the mirror. She was bewildered to find she still had brown eyes. And then she felt the Lord gave her an explanation: sometimes the answer is no. At a very early age, she learned a profound, hard lesson about the nature of prayer.

When she was twelve, Amy was sent to a Wesleyan Methodist boarding school in Harrogate, Yorkshire. She was homesick but did not question her parents' decision. Amy didn't particularly like Marlborough House boarding school, but at the end of the three years she experienced a watershed moment. One evening, there was a children's special service in Harrogate. While singing the famous hymn "Jesus Loves Me," Amy realized that there was much work to be done in the world. She always knew of Jesus' love, but in those quiet moments at age fifteen, she knew God was requiring more of her. There, she surrendered her whole life to His service.

Around that time, for business reasons, the Carmichaels moved to Belfast. Financial difficulties forced the parents to remove all the children from boarding school. The Carmichaels never discussed money struggles in front of the children, but later Amy learned that her father lent several thousands of pounds to a friend who was not able to pay him back.

It was during that time that her father contracted double pneumonia. He died at age fifty-four. Amy didn't seem to question that this was God's best for her father and her family. She trusted God and knew He would take care of them. Her mother found solace in Nahum 1:7: "The LORD is good, a strong hold in the day of trouble; and he knoweth them that trust in him" (KJV). Amy followed her mother's example. Instead of becoming angry and resentful toward God, she threw herself into serving others. Her sisters learned from Amy's enthusiasm and benefited from her knowledge and hunger for beauty. Amy was not preoccupied with her looks, her clothing, or her social life like most seventeen-year-old girls. Her sensitivity toward others was evident in her actions.

One dull, rainy Sunday afternoon she was returning from church with her family. She and her brothers saw an old woman carrying a heavy load down the streets of Belfast. They didn't know her situation but went to help the woman, despite the stares from other Christians on their way home.

The harsh wind was blowing through them, and the drizzling rain drenched the woman's bundle of old rags. Amy tried to ignore the looks and comments of others who disapproved of their helping a lower-class citizen. Suddenly, in her mind's eye she caught a glimpse of an ornate Victorian fountain and the words of 1 Corinthians 3:12–14 flashed before her: "Now if any man build upon this foundation gold, silver, precious stones, wood, hay, stubble; every man's work shall be made manifest: for the day shall declare it, because it shall be revealed by fire; and the fire shall try every man's work of what sort it is. If any man's work abide which he hath built thereupon, he shall receive a reward."

Amy knew the words were for her, and at home she shut herself in her room to settle her heart before God.

Soon, Amy began holding neighborhood meetings for children, encouraging them to read their Bibles daily and spend time in prayer. Amy also worked at the YWCA, helping the "shawlies" (women who could not afford hats to cover their heads and so instead wore shawls) learn about God's love for them. Amy's church members criticized Mrs. Carmichael for letting her daughter associate with the lower class and venture to the slums to get them and bring them home for ministry.

But Amy poured herself into the lives of the children in her neighborhood and into the shawlies. She knew she was sheltered and was not aware of all the world's evils. While she tried to do all she could for others, she felt it wasn't enough. She wanted to serve more. She wanted more of God.

The number of shawlies coming to the neighborhood disturbed Amy's community. They were uncomfortable with so many of the lower class invading their streets. Amy knew she needed to find a building to accommodate them. In a magazine advertisement, she learned she could construct an iron building for five hundred pounds. That was an awesome sum of money, and Amy knew she needed the Lord's help.

Amy and the shawlies began to pray faithfully for the funds and were rewarded when an older woman with ample finances sent word to Amy telling her she would fund the hall she needed. The iron tabernacle was a lively place, and the shawlies enjoyed Bible studies, singing classes, and prayer meetings because of Amy's desire to serve.

Amy soon moved to the slums to help women around the clock. She heard the brawls and screams of desperation each night. In the day she heard the factory sirens and the heavy footsteps of the working class trudging to work. She learned to do without privacy and quiet and was not afraid to walk alone, even in the dangerous parts of the city.

Though Amy enjoyed her work with the factory girls, on January 13, 1892, God told the young woman it was time to leave. She was torn, as she felt she was needed there. Yet, clear as a human voice, she heard "Go ye." Through the struggle of leaving family and enduring others' criticism, Amy faithfully determined to go to the mission field.

She went on to spend fifty-three years in South India without furlough. She became known as *Amma*, which means "mother." There, she founded the Dohnavur Fellowship, which was a refuge for hundreds of children who were secretly set aside for Hindu temple prostitution. Amma was greatly loved at Dohnavur and resolved to give all of her life to save the children.

Throughout her life of service, Amy's silent offerings, unseen struggles, and steady obedience made those around her wonder if she was some sort of angel or saint. But Amy knew her humanity was what God could use to fulfill her calling. She wrote, "Teach us, good Lord, to serve Thee as Thou deservest; to give and not to count the cost; to fight and not to heed the wounds; to toil and not to seek for rest; to labor and not to ask for any reward save that of knowing that we do Thy will, O Lord our God."

Amy was willing to serve.

[Christ Jesus] Who, being in very nature God,
*   did not consider equality with God something to be grasped,*
but made himself nothing,
*   taking the very nature of a servant,*
being made in human likeness.
*   And being found in appearance as a man,*
he humbled himself and became obedient to death—
*   even death on a cross!*

(Philippians 2:5–8)

Kate
FREE FROM FEAR

I am confident of this: God has never abandoned, and will never abandon, me. For most of her life, Kate doubted this truth. Certain that hurt was coming her way, she set out to protect her heart. She believed friends and family eventually would abandon her, so somehow God would too.

Kate's fear didn't make any rational sense—she knew that. She had a home that was the envy of others. Her parents were loving and devoted Christians. Yet Kate's heart sank every time her father pulled out of the driveway for a business trip. *Will he come back?* she'd think. *No. No, he won't—I'm sure of it.*

Kate doesn't know how all this started, but as she grew so did her fear that she would be alone. By junior high she wasn't spending any time developing friendships; it was far too risky. Without any friends to distract her, she threw herself into her studies. Her 4.0 GPA proved she was self-sufficient and safe, she thought. Kate graduated from junior high with the highest marks in her class, but not one friend.

Even though Kate had been busy closing herself off, she had a tiny vulnerable spot: she wanted to be liked. She wanted to sit in the lunchroom with other kids and laugh. She wanted to be understood. At the start of her freshman year of high school, Kate joined the drama team. Fortunately, it came with a ready-made group of friends. In fact, most of her new drama cohorts were upperclassmen. Kate began to open up just a little.

As the semester progressed, she dropped her defenses one by one. She let down her guard in every area except dating. That was still too scary, and Kate wasn't sure she should be dating at that point in her life anyway. Not a big deal. But her friends noticed and a rumor started. Soon all her newfound "friends" had heard the gossip and started questioning, "Are you really gay?" No matter how much Kate protested, the questions-turned-accusations continued. Snapping shut again, she felt abused, misunderstood . . . and abandoned.

As the months passed, Kate's anger grew. It seemed obvious God couldn't fix this one. Determined to stop the rumor, she took it into her own hands. She became obsessed with finding a boyfriend. You can imagine her shock at her success when within a few weeks three boys expressed interest. *Finally,* Kate thought, *this whole mess will go away.* But, for some reason, none of them ever asked her out. Her new label seemed as if it would never be erased.

One day, she went home, slammed her door, and turned her rage on God: "Why are You letting this happen to me? The solution is so simple! I need a boyfriend! Why can't You come through for me just this once?"

A few days later Kate realized God *had* come through for her—big-time. A friend told her that two of the boys who had been flirting with her had been asking out lots of freshman girls. All they were interested in was "getting some." Kate sat stunned and humbled. She realized, *My heavenly Father's hand has been on me all along. He has not gone on a business trip; He has been busy building a hedge of protection around me.*

Things started looking up, and during her sophomore year in high school a Bible study began to meet at Kate's house. She thought her heart would be safe if she surrounded herself with other Christians. Unfortunately, it doesn't always happen that way. One day Kate was asked to help resolve a conflict between two of the students, Rob and Lara. She was glad to help. She dug up Scripture that applied and gave her findings to Rob. The whole situation ended up spinning out of control and Lara's group of friends left the Bible study—furious with Kate.

She cried out to God: "I can't do this anymore. I can't keep on putting myself out there just to be hurt and rejected!" Kate had already forgotten God doesn't forsake His children.

At the end of her sophomore year, Kate's parents persuaded her to go on a short-term mission trip to Quito, Ecuador. She couldn't see how God could use her in Ecuador if He couldn't even use her at home. Kate would soon realize that God's plan in sending her wasn't to "use her" but rather to bind up her broken heart. Kate's heavenly Father wanted to set her free from all her strategies. There was a plan behind her hurt. God wanted to demonstrate to her that He would never leave her or turn her away.

Within the first two weeks, God provided Kate with fast friendships with other girls on the trip. She had never felt so loved and accepted by a peer group. Kate slowly began to realize she had stopped loving people and was relying on judgment and anger for comfort. Through this new experience God was teaching her how to "be joyful in hope, patient in affliction, and faithful in prayer" (Rom. 12:12).

But Kate's trials didn't stop. When she returned to school, her reputation as a prude continued to grow. One day at lunch a girl Kate always sat with taunted, "You know you're going to break, Kate. The longer you try to hold out, the wilder you're going to get. You're probably going to be a porn star."

Kate cringed at the thought. The girl obviously didn't understand that Kate's decision not to date wasn't due to some tremendously repressed passion but to her growing love for God. She was determined not to allow her healed heart to be broken again by anger and bitterness.

Kate's newfound assurance in God's faithfulness must have disappointed Satan. Perhaps the devil thought if he sent more pain her way, she would crumple and accuse God of leaving her. She got hit again the next day. A group of kids got on the porn-star kick and began drawing up cartoons of her in her "new profession." Amazingly, God shielded Kate's heart from Satan's filthy attack.

Around the same time, another "friend" began publicly ridiculing Kate for being a Christian. She poked fun at Kate's faith and her obvious stupidity for believing anything so base. God had already carried her through a lot in high school. So, that time Kate stood firm with His hand on her shoulder. Kate began to see how far she'd come in trusting her closest and dearest Friend.

Kate wasn't exactly persecuted for her faith at school, but she regretted that she was closed off and angry for so long. It also saddens her to think that girls don't recognize how damaging gossip can be. Still, she doesn't regret the pain and frustration she endured. Because of it, Kate knows God is with her no matter where she is or what she's doing. Kate is safe. God is closer to her than her breath. And today Kate is certain of this:

God is her shield of protection when accusations and insults are thrown her way. He is the Protector of her heart.

———•——— ———•——— ———•——— ———•——— ———•——— ———•———

If anyone loves me, he will obey my teaching. My Father will love him, and we will come to him and make our home with him.

(John 14:23)

———•——— ———•——— ———•——— ———•——— ———•——— ———•———

crystal rains

ALLIES FOR CHRIST

allies *n. pl.* 1. Those who are united with others in friendship or relationship. 2. Those that come together for a common purpose and shared goal.

Crystal Rains had enjoyed a couple of amazing summers as part of a high-powered summer camp. Revival seemed to be a daily occurrence with students responding to energized worship and messages about salvation. Then, toward the end of her second summer, between her junior and senior years in high school, God began to stir something new in her soul.

At first it was just an idea. But then the idea began to grow. While Crystal had seen many come to Christ at camp, her thoughts began to turn back home. "A compelling passion for my lost friends pulled me to my knees in prayer," she says. "I couldn't really stop it, even if I'd wanted to."

As she prayed, the idea began to expand until it was far bigger than she was—but in no way bigger than the God she knew. By the time the camps were over, her idea had become a vision. Crystal knew what she needed to do: one way or another, she wanted to see every middle school and high school student in her city have an opportunity to hear about Christ. She just wasn't sure how she was going to do it.

Back home, she began to talk with her close friend, Renee. "She was immediately excited. We had been leading an on-campus Christian club at our high school called Allies. This new passion seemed like a natural, yet much bigger, extension of what we were already doing. It was scary, but we felt God telling us we needed to try."

But there were plenty of obstacles. For starters, the city where they lived was divided by a mountain, which pushed the city into an east side and west side. Each side had its own high school and several middle schools. The mountain was not the biggest barrier, however. A bitter rivalry between the schools had recently erupted into fights and vandalism. Several students ended up in the hospital, others landed in jail. One weekend, the administration canceled a football game and other activities for fear of more east-west violence. If Crystal's vision was to become a reality, she would need to build a bridge over the mountain, across the prejudice, and through the violence.

Crystal, an "east-sider," had one connection on the other side of town—a friend named Nick. On the day she called him, he just happened to be meeting with Drew and Timmi, the other leaders of the Allies from the west side. "That alone seemed to be an amazing 'coincidence,'" Crystal said. "By the end of that phone call, everyone was all for it." The Allies from each school came together as a single team. United with one desire, they would give every student in town an opportunity to hear about Jesus.

They planned to begin by mobilizing citywide prayer and support through churches, then launch three citywide rallies where students could come and hear the gospel. "Through prayer and compromise we made it happen," Nick said. "We had to learn to flex and forgive like never before. We had to respect and rely on each other's gifts and skills."

First they needed a name for their outreach. The city's youth were in trouble. Suicide and drug abuse had taken the lives of several students the year before. Rape and alcoholism were draining the life out of many, many others. Therefore, the Allies decided to call their plan Desperate for God, because that was exactly what their city was.

The first rally was a mobilization event for other Christians. It was packed in the school's theater that night. God was raising up an army of youth groups behind the Allies, and the word began to spread. The second rally exceeded everyone's dreams. Every seat in the auditorium was taken, the band was awesome, and when the speaker gave an invitation to receive Christ, the aisles filled. As students walked down front, tears streamed down Timmi's face. She held the door open for them to enter the counseling room, where they opened the doors of their hearts to Christ. It was an amazing night, and the whole plan seemed to be right on track.

"We needed to raise over fifteen thousand dollars to cover all our expenses," Crystal recalls. "One day, we were short a thousand dollars to pay a band. That day a man came into a church and donated just the right amount to make the payment. It was one of those stories about God's faithfulness that you read about, but it was our story."

In May, however, just before the third and largest Desperate for God rally, every one of the Allies was under pressure. Crystal seemed to be struggling the most. "It was a huge mental and spiritual battle. In my own heart I was fighting insecurities and physical temptation with my boyfriend. I kept thinking, *I don't have time to struggle like this! I'm supposed to be a leader. I can't do it!* Two days before the rally I went to the park alone and completely broke down before the Lord, repented of my selfishness, and gave my struggles to Him. It was a small breakthrough, and I left feeling God would be sufficient in whatever came our way."

On the morning of the final rally, a heavy cloud seemed to hang over the team. "We read together from the Psalms, and that gave us some hope. We prayed and believed, but we didn't 'feel' much peace. We clung to His words, but we still felt only tension and stress. I had never experienced spiritual opposition like that before," Crystal says.

During the setup, the sound system blew fuses and the lights didn't work. The stage crew was having lots of trouble, and arguments flared up. When the band members flew in, they were tired, frustrated, and angry—and that night their music sounded like it. A special evangelist flew in, but when he spoke, his words seemed to bounce off the walls, echoing without meaning in the hollow gym. As he began to make an invitation to come to Christ, several groups of students headed for the door.

But then something happened—something beyond what could be seen, beyond all that had been done, beyond the bands and the lights and all the money that had been given. God began to touch desperate hearts with His Spirit, and slowly, one by one, students came forward to give their lives to Him. The floor of the gym was crowded that night with students. Those who came with a need left with eternal life.

"That's when I knew this was all about Him and not about the Allies," says Crystal. "He had chosen us for His service and brought us together that year for a specific purpose. He was the one who was at work, not us."

How many students did the Allies reach that year? Only God knows for sure. All we can tell from this side of heaven is that the world and eternity will be different because one young woman listened, prayed, and obeyed—and then saw God build a team of allies who invested their senior year of high school in something that would last forever.

———

In your hearts set apart Christ as Lord. Always be prepared to give an answer to everyone who asks you to give the reason for the hope that you have.

(1 Peter 3:15)

———

WEEK FOUR JOURNAL

—◆—

⇥ If God were to ask you to take a major step of faith, what might it be?

⇥ Right now, where could you be investing your time, energy, and creativity in things that will last for eternity?

⇥ What kinds of "allies" has God placed around you?

⇥ How could you work together with others to fulfill a common vision?

⇥ What Bible verse or passage of Scripture has been most meaningful to you this week? Why?

Manche Masemola

A LIFE OF FAITH

She never went to school. Born in poverty in 1911, Manche Masemola was too busy working on her family's farm (if the barren piece of dirt in what is now South Africa could be called that) for formal education. Manche and her family, along with the other members of her Pedi tribe, were confined to a reservation that barely produced enough food to keep them alive. It was not until she was a teenager that Manche first entered a classroom.

In 1927, when Manche was fifteen or sixteen, Christian missionaries were just starting to reach the Transvaal, where Manche lived with her parents; two older brothers; a younger sister, Mabule; and her cousin, Lucia. One evening after the work was done, Manche and Lucia walked several miles to an evangelistic service, where Manche heard Father Augustine Moeka share the message of the gospel for the first time. That night, she accepted Jesus' love and forgiveness, and she became a Christian.

After her conversion, Manche traveled twice a week to Father Moeka's mission in the nearby town of Marishane to study the Bible and prepare for baptism. When her parents found out about her new faith, though, they were angry. The Pedi people were suspicious of Christianity, which had been brought to the region by the same Europeans who forced them to live on the reservation. Most Pedis held onto the pagan faith and traditions of their ancestors. Manche's parents feared that their daughter's new religion would bring shame to their family, especially if Manche refused to marry the man from her tribe that her mother and father had chosen to be her husband.

Manche's mother told her that she could not attend the Bible classes anymore, but Manche went anyway. By the fall of 1927, her parents realized that words alone would not influence their headstrong daughter, and they began to beat her severely, sometimes twice a day. "Manche's mother said she would force us to leave the church. She beat Manche every time she returned from church," Lucia said later. Concerned that the Pedi gods would punish the entire family for their daughter's choice, Manche's mother became so angry that she even attacked Manche once with a spear.

But Manche's faith was stronger than any fear she may have had. She continued to defy her parents by going to church and attending classes for baptism, an important sign of faith to the Anglican church.

Despite her persistence, Manche seemed to know she would never complete her classes. "I will be baptized in my own blood," she told Father Moeka. She believed that her parents' abuse would eventually kill her, and she shared her fears with both the priest and her cousin. Yet she continued to travel to Father Moeka's mission for class and professed her Christian faith openly to the people around her.

In February 1928, her mother had grown desperate to make Manche renounce her Christianity and return to the faith of her ancestors. On the morning of one of Manche's baptism classes, the older woman hid all of her daughter's clothes to try to prevent her from going. Although she was naked, Manche fled the house and hid in the barren brushland. Her mother and father searched the hills around the house until they found her. When they did, her parents called a *sangoma,* a spirit priest, and told him their daughter was bewitched. The witch doctor tried to make Manche drink a traditional potion to rid her of the evil spirits her parents believed were controlling her. When she refused, Manche's mother beat her severely and forced the vile substance down the girl's throat.

"They went on beating her till she drank it. Then she died," Lucia reported.

It is not clear whether Manche died that day from the medicine or the beating. Her parents left her body in the remote wilderness, burying her beside a granite rock. Although everyone knew and talked about what had happened to the young Christian girl, her mother and father were never punished for taking the life of their daughter.

A few days after Manche died, her younger sister, Mabule, became ill, and although no one could find out what was wrong with her, she died at the local mission. Her parents buried her near her sister, and the girls' father planted several native euphorbia shade trees near their graves to mark the site.

Tales of Manche's faith and suffering spread, and seven years after her death, a group of Christians traveled to her gravesite to pay their respects. Another group came a few years later, and after that more and more Christians made the pilgrimage to the South African wilderness to honor the brave Christian girl. Her story became the foundation on which many African churches were founded, and many people came to know Christ because of Manche's sacrifice.

In honor of her commitment, the Anglican church recognizes Manche Masemola every year on the anniversary of the day she died, February 4. In 1998, an almost life-size statue of Manche was unveiled with a group of twentieth-century martyrs above a door in the famous Westminster Abbey in London, England.

Perhaps more importantly, though, forty years after Manche's death, her mother accepted Jesus as her Savior and was baptized, in part because of the witness of her daughter. Manche Masemola—young, uneducated, and raised in extreme poverty—continues to serve as a testimony to what the simple faith and single-minded determination of one girl can accomplish.

LORD, who may dwell in your sanctuary?
   Who may live on your holy hill?
He whose walk is blameless
   and who does what is righteous.

(Psalm 15:1–2)

janine ramer
SPEAKING THE TRUTH

Whenever people in Dalton, Ohio, think about Janine Ramer, the first thing most remember is her smile.

When the popular, active high-school junior died tragically, she left her friends, family, and neighbors plenty to remember. She was president of her class, a varsity cheerleader, member of the National Honor Society, a cross-country runner, and an active church youth group leader. She played softball, participated in short-term mission trips, and maintained an almost 4.0 grade-point average.

More important, Janine was a committed Christian and one of the nicest girls anyone—classmates or adults—ever met. "I've probably coached six hundred kids in thirty years," softball coach George Strong says, his voice catching as he thinks about the bright, energetic girl who lit up his team for two years. "I never coached one like her. She never had a cross word for anyone. She never saw a negative in anyone."

Janine's parents, Keith and Florence, remember their youngest daughter a little differently; Flo describes Janine as a normal, happy girl who naturally was bothered by some things. "Of course she had down days. She would be upset if she didn't get enough playing time [on the field], but she didn't let it show. In the long run, she realized that's not what really mattered."

What did matter to Janine was serving Jesus. She accepted Christ as her Savior when she was young and grew up attending and participating in church regularly. But Janine's faith was deeper than just getting together with the youth group kids or going to a worship service on Sundays. She was passionate about her personal relationship with Christ and committed to growing as a Christian.

When her parents looked through her well-marked Bible after her death, they found part of Psalm 119 highlighted. They don't know if Janine saw these words as her life-defining Scripture, but looking back, the verses seem to reflect who she was and how she lived: "How can a young man [or young woman] keep his [or her] way pure? / By living according to your word. / I seek you with all my heart; / Do not let me stray from your commands" (vv. 9–10).

Janine seemed to understand instinctively that the best way to bring others to Christ was not to preach at them, but to show them the love of Christ. "She didn't push Christ; she wasn't nagging," her mother explains. "She was just always caring about other people. People could feel her care."

If a classmate or friend seemed interested, Janine invited that person to her church's monthly evangelistic service. But mostly, she just loved everyone around her. She saw her life as a mission field and looked for ways to bring her Christian faith into conversations.

When Janine first considered joining a traveling softball team, she hesitated. The team often played games on Sundays, and she would have to miss church. She talked about the situation with her parents and her youth pastor, and they encouraged her to play and to look at softball as a mission field. Janine took their challenge seriously. When her team went to represent its division in the World Series, she asked her pastor to pray that she would have the chance to introduce Christ to some of her teammates. She never even mentioned the game.

Her passion for Christ and her commitment to ministry brought Janine to a ceremony honoring her youth leaders on a cold January night in 2003. "She had fourteen thousand other things to do," her mentor and junior-high youth pastor, Dave Graber, says. "She didn't have time to serve us, but she did."

Janine and several other members of the youth group waited tables while the attendees ate, then took turns sharing their own testimonies and future plans. When it was Janine's turn, she sat on a stool at the front of the room and spoke from her heart. Dave remembers, "She talked about her passion for serving Christ. She told us she wanted to be a youth leader— maybe not a youth pastor, but definitely someone who works with youth and helps teens understand who Christ is."

When she was done speaking, Janine slipped on her coat and left the ceremony early; she still had homework to do. Less than a half mile from the banquet, as she drove through an intersection, a tractor-trailer with faulty brakes ran a red light and hit her car on the driver's door. Paramedics rushed her to the hospital and did everything they could, but she never responded to medical treatment. Janine probably died instantly.

The entire community mourned with the Ramers. Keith and Florence stood in the receiving line for more than ten hours as hundreds of people waited in the frigid Midwest winter night to share their sympathy with the family. Some of them knew Janine well. Some she had met only once. But Janine was a person who affected people, even in the briefest meetings.

Even in death, Janine's passion for Christ changed lives. George, her softball coach, struggled with the sudden loss of his favorite player, but he found comfort listening to Janine's pastor during her memorial service. George began to understand that this positive, generous girl had seemed so different because of her relationship with Jesus Christ. George started to attend the Ramers' church and eventually became a Christian because of Janine's influence on his life. "I always believed in God, but I wasn't a very religious person," George explains now. "I know that Janine's in heaven, and [becoming a Christian] is the way that I will get to see her in heaven someday and say thank you."

Janine's youth group also looked for positive ways to remember her. As they grieved together, one of the stories about Janine that came up over and over was the way she "met Ray Jameson." A few years before her death, Janine had traveled to Colorado with several members of the youth group for a national youth convention. Goofing around between the sessions, Janine decided to meet people. She walked up to a complete stranger, another conference attendee, and pretended to think he was "Ray Jameson," her long-lost friend. She pulled it off so well, and so kindly, that the conference attendee appreciated the joke and became friends with the kids from Ohio.

After her death, a leader in Janine's youth group launched the Ray Jameson Project. In honor of Janine's outgoing nature, the church now trains student leaders to strike up conversations with strangers in malls or other public places and guide the discussion to spiritual topics.

Throughout high school, Janine kept a journal that chronicled her spiritual life. When her parents read it after her death, they found a quote that Janine copied from somewhere. It seemed to accurately sum up the way the passionate sixteen-year-old lived her life: "Lots of people may have lots of opinions about you, but you're only playing for an audience of one."

Janine Ramer lived so well for her audience of One that she changed a community.

I rejoice in following your statutes,
*   as one rejoices in great riches.*
I meditate on your precepts
*   and consider your ways.*
I delight in your decrees;
*   I will not neglect your word.*

(Psalm 119:14–16)

jaime haidle

OVERCOMING INSECURITY

For as long as she could remember, Jaime Haidle's mind was a giant aqueduct, filled to the brim with other people's thoughts. At times she was so consumed with what *others* were thinking about her that she couldn't tell what *she* was thinking. Worry and tension were her constant companions.

From the very start, Jaime was a perfectionist, afraid to mess up in any way. She questioned the purpose of life, and her life in particular. Why was she on earth? She wasn't sure, but she felt that she must do it right—no, perfectly.

Jaime made a decision before her sophomore year of college that no matter what, she was going to make God a priority in her life. Jaime had grown up in a mainline church, focused on repetition and good deeds, and she believed these were important in serving Him faithfully. She wanted to please God as well as everyone else.

Jaime met Chrisy, a Christian who went to weekly meetings of Campus Crusade for Christ (a national student group with chapters at many colleges and universities). With Jaime's new commitment to pursue God, she decided to go with Chrisy every week.

During one of the first meetings of the year, they talked about Jesus and having a personal relationship with Him. At the end the speaker said that maybe some of the audience had never asked Jesus to be a part of their lives, and they could do that right then. That night Jaime confessed that she was a sinner and needed Him.

Things began to change. For starters, Jaime was stunned at hearing God's Word come alive. In her old church, the Bible seemed like a set of good principles, but Jaime was learning that the Word had significance for her every day. She was blown away.

Jaime was excited about her new relationship with the Lord, but insecurities still consumed her. During her freshman year of college, she had gained about thirty pounds, and soon unhealthy eating habits began to control her emotions. Jaime *constantly* thought about what she looked like. She had such a terrible self-image that she didn't want to walk across campus for fear that someone would recognize her. Jaime tried talking with her mom about her weight and concern about food, but her mom couldn't recognize the depth of Jaime's struggle. Repeatedly she said, "Oh Jaime, stop. It's like you are obsessed."

Jaime *was* obsessed!

In reality she wasn't fat, but she truly *was* haunted by her lack of control. Jaime even snuck into her roommates' food. One night she ate almost an entire bag of gingersnaps. She felt sick and undone emotionally. Jaime had been binge eating for a while, but that one night was particularly horrible. She called her mom, sobbing that she had a problem.

That week Jaime began going to a nutritionist and a counselor on campus. Her eating habits soon became normal again, but her thought life was still a losing battle. Jaime's insecurities began to hinder her ability to make friendships and reach out to others. Even though she felt worthless much of the time, God continued to work in her life.

At a Christmas conference that year, Jaime was challenged to spend time with the Lord in prayer and in the Bible. She also heard about summer projects in which college students move to a resort area, form new friendships, and receive training and discipleship. Jaime tucked away the idea in the back of her mind.

All that next spring semester, she enjoyed having her first quiet times with the Lord. Jaime loved her new relationship with God. During this time, He kept nudging the young woman toward a summer project. But all the while, she continued to struggle terribly with her body image. She had given Jesus her life, but she couldn't trust Him with her eating and desire to lose weight. Jaime just felt the whole thing was too vain and unimportant. Why would God want to answer her prayer to lose weight?

Jaime grew excited about the upcoming summer project but was nervous that her obsessive thoughts would distract her. She marveled at how on one hand, she could experience victory, but on the other, she still was losing other battles. The night before she left, Jaime pleaded with the Lord to change all her thoughts from food and her body to Him: "Holy Fire, burn away my desire for anything that is not of You and is of me. I want more of You and less of me. Empty me and fill me with You. Jesus, only You truly satisfy."

God answered Jaime's prayer! She saw firsthand His ability to bring victory over that huge stronghold. She was able to go on the project and completely focus on the Lord. Still, in light of all He had done for her, the idea of having confidence still seemed impossible. In desperation, Jaime studied the characteristics of God and what He said about His children.

Jaime started learning how to share her faith. On her first outreach, she was so nervous she was sick to her stomach. She remembers seeing the bathroom in the distance, wishing she could run and hide in there for the rest of the day. Later that day, she was having a quiet time at a picnic table when the Lord prompted her to go over and talk to a girl.

Finally Jaime obeyed and introduced herself to Lana. Jaime explained about why she was in Lake Tahoe and asked if Lana would read a little booklet with her. When she finished, Lana said the message was exactly what she had been looking for. She had actually been meeting with a cult and was about to join. She recognized this message was different and true, and she thanked Jaime for talking to her.

The Holy Spirit's work overwhelmed Jaime, and she realized that sharing the gospel was something God had called her to do for the rest of her life, no matter how scary it seemed.

Most of the time these days, Jaime just feels swept away with Him, trying to keep up with what He is doing through her. She even moved back into the dorms, where He's used her to reach out to incoming freshmen. Jaime also got the chance to share the gospel with some Japanese students throughout the year, and the following spring God sent her on a mission trip to Japan.

All the while, Jaime has learned she must daily lay down her need to be perfect, rejecting such thoughts as: *I need to pray more, share my faith more, have greater faith, love God more.*

She continues to pray that God will reveal and heal her unhealthy ideas. He's shown Jaime that she is still in process.

She's always known intellectually that God loved her, but she has found it difficult to accept His profound love for her apart from her servanthood.

Is she sold out for Jesus? You bet. But for Jaime that is the easy part. She's still on a more difficult journey in her heart: learning to believe Jesus is sold out for her too.

You then, my son, be strong in the grace that is in Christ Jesus. And the things you have heard me say in the presence of many witnesses, entrust to reliable men who will also be qualified to teach others.

(2 Timothy 2:1–2)

perpetua and felicitas
GIVING THEIR ALL

The time was around AD 200 in North Africa. Rome was under the rule of Septimus Severus. As emperor, he proposed to bring all citizens under syncretism, which meant the acceptance of all gods under the worship of *Sol invictus*—the Unconquered Sun. But two groups would not conform to this type of religion: Jews and Christians. Severus decided to stop the spread of both, and persecution of Christians (as well as Jews) quickly increased.

But within this religious culture a strong Christian community existed. Perpetua, a young, educated, well-to-do woman, had become a Christian. She lived with her husband, her infant son, and her beloved slave, Felicitas, in Carthage.

Though she was still nursing her infant son, Perpetua and Felicitas were arrested by Roman officials, who threw them into prison. Quickly, Perpetua's father went to rescue her. He knew she was in danger of losing her life and that there was an easy escape: deny she was a Christian.

She responded, "Father, do you see this vase here?"

"Yes, I do."

"Could it be called by any other name than what it is?"

"No."

"I cannot be called anything other than what I am—a Christian."

The word angered her father. He pleaded, "Think of your mother, your brother, your aunt. Please, Perpetua, think of me, your aging father. But most of all, think of your little baby!"

She agonized over her father's pain, but she knew there was no turning back. Young women did not deny their fathers' pleas in that patriarchal society. Perpetua's choice to remain faithful to God had disgraced her family. Finally, her father left her and Felicitas to suffer the consequences of their decision: being devoured by beasts.

Two deacons, Tertius and Pomponius, tried to take care of Perpetua and Felicitas while they awaited their death sentence. The two men bribed the prison soldiers to give Perpetua permission to nurse her baby. The young mother wrote in her journal: "My prison had suddenly become a palace, so that I wanted to be there rather than anywhere else."

Felicitas was expecting a child at the time of the arrest. During her eighth month of pregnancy, the faithful slave gave birth. She told the jailers, "Now my sufferings are only mine. But when I face the beasts there will be another who will live in me, and will suffer for me since I shall be suffering for him." Providentially, Felicitas's child was adopted by a Christian woman.

Perpetua saw the profound grief her decision was causing her brother. He said, "Dear sister, you are greatly privileged; surely you might ask for a vision to discover whether you are to be condemned or freed." Faithfully, she asked the Lord for a vision.

She then saw a bronze ladder reaching to the heavens. It was narrow and looked as if only one person could climb the steps. On the side of the ladder were many weapons—swords, spears, hooks, and spikes. Perpetua knew that if she were to try to climb the ladder without caution and care, she would be mangled. At the bottom of the ladder lay a dragon, waiting to attack anyone who would try and climb the ladder. Perpetua then saw Saturus, the mentor who taught her about Christianity, beckoning her to follow him to the heavens. She sensed the dragon was afraid of her and dreaded her strength. Once she had witnessed this vision, she told her brother that she believed she must suffer for the faith and not go free.

One morning, Roman guards hurried Perpetua and Felicitas to their hearing. Her father appeared, pleading with her one final time to have mercy on her baby and burn incense to the gods. The governor asked Perpetua to have pity on her father and offer the sacrifice for the welfare of her family.

"I will not!" she vehemently cried.

"Are you a Christian?" asked the governor.

"Yes, I am."

When her father continued to plead for Perpetua to renounce her faith, the governor ordered her father to be beaten. She felt as if the blows actually landed on her body. Finally, Perpetua and Felicitus were condemned to the beasts. They returned to their cell knowing their sentence, yet in high spirits.

On March 7, 203, marching to the amphitheater with calm hearts, the women trembled with joy rather than fear. Perpetua's countenance was one of peace, testifying to her love for God. The two sisters in Christ were led to the gates, where they were forced to wear the robes of the god Ceres. Perpetua begged for the freedom to declare Jesus as Lord. The officials finally complied with her request and she began to sing hymns to the Lord, rejoicing that she had fellowship with the sufferings of Christ.

The two young women were stripped naked, and the officials set loose a mad heifer to devour their flesh. The crowd was horrified to see that a young girl and a nursing mother were to die, so the officials gave them tunics to cover their bodies.

The mad animal violently tossed Perpetua and crushed Felicitas. The Christian men to be martyred entered the stadium, and Perpetua encouraged them to stand strong to the end despite the savage death they faced.

Shortly after the death of these women, Christian persecution subsided for a time. Perhaps the Roman world glimpsed its own savagery and was repelled by the cruelty of the human heart. Maybe the spectators who witnessed the testimony of the young women saw a glimpse of Jesus as the windows of heaven opened and He welcomed them with loving arms.

I have been crucified with Christ and I no longer live, but Christ lives in me. The life I live in the body, I live by faith in the Son of God, who loved me and gave himself for me.

(Galatians 2:20)

---

karen myers
NOT GUILTY

Wichita's newspaper headline read, "Abortion Protester Vindicated in Jury Trial."

Karen Myers was among a small group of protesters holding signs in the grassy pedestrian right-of-way outside the local coliseum entrance on March 14, 2003. Karen had been going to abortion clinics since she was about six years old. Her dad made cardboard signs to string around Karen and her siblings' necks that said, "We are glad to be alive." This was an every-Saturday event for the Myers family. Even at her young age, Karen knew people were changing their minds and babies were being saved just from reading their signs.

Her grandmother, Ellen Myers, was a cofounder of Right to Life of Kansas, a pro-life organization formed in 1969 even before Kansas legalized abortion. Ellen, a survivor of the Holocaust who became a Christian when she came to America, saw the same evils in the act of abortion.

Karen says, "When I was five years old, I saw a picture of an actual aborted baby. I knew it was wrong even then. My mom and dad aren't the kind of parents who hide things from their kids. They told us about abortion and that it was wrong."

March 13 started out like many other nights Karen had participated in. Karen always arrived at the designated venue an hour or so before an event or concert to engage in outreach. That night, Cher, a strong voice for a woman's right to choose, would be performing at the coliseum. The poster in Karen's hand read, "Hurting after abortion? Call us!"

Suddenly a deputy shouted, "Move one hundred feet back!" Without warning, Karen felt him twist her arms twice into a double hammerlock. As he jerked her back and forth, she felt as if her arms were being torn off. She begged him to stop hurting her.

Then he slammed Karen to the ground, pushing all of his weight against her small-framed body, smashing her face into the dirt. The deputy didn't read her rights or indicate he was arresting her. Karen was unsure of what was really happening. She cried out in pain. Were her arms broken, or dislocated?

Fiery sensations ran up and down her shoulders, and she knew she was injured. Deputy Simpson dragged Karen over to the landscaped entrance of the coliseum. She begged that paramedics be called, as her arms continued to swell and throb. With dried dirt and tears covering her cheeks, she waited an hour for medical help, watching the concert spectators pass her, staring. But in those moments, Karen felt the presence of Jesus with her as never before.

Karen eventually was allowed to go home. Ten months passed, and she attended another pro-life outreach. Officials said it was perfectly legal to be there but asked to run a routine ID record check on everyone present. Karen was shocked to learn there was a warrant out for her arrest. Deputy Simpson had filed charges against her five months after the concert without telling her. She had no idea she had committed any kind of violation.

After receiving counsel, Karen decided to turn herself over to the authorities, even though she was not guilty. It was a horrible afternoon. Placed in a large holding cell, Karen took the opportunity to witness to the other women there. The guards didn't like that and pulled her out to harass her. Sexual innuendo and perverse language filled the air. Then they placed her alone in a four-by-four-foot cell, where she had room only to stand. The cell reeked of excrement and vomit. It was a long four hours.

Finally, Karen got a trial date, although she never received a standard hearing first. She tried to get answers about her wrongful arrest. After she made many calls to Christian lawyers, none agreed to represent Karen in court. The case was against the county, they said, and it was risky. "You won't win" kept ringing in her ears.

Karen tried to formally file an assault-and-battery charge against Deputy Simpson but was told she could not do so. The injuries to her arms caused such severe pain that she had to quit her job. Emotional scars, such as panic attacks and nightmares, haunted her. Phone call after phone call, she sought justice by talking with lawyers and legal advisors.

Out of desperation, Karen finally called a contract lawyer. He knew a criminal defense attorney who agreed to help fight the county. An out-of-state Christian legal group promised to assist.

Seventeen months after the assault, Karen went to trial. Relieved, yet apprehensive about reliving the trauma of the event, she faced the jury, knowing two members were strong abortion advocates. The horror of the night of the Cher concert came flooding back and Karen had to compose herself to respond to the questions and interrogation. She knew lots of people were praying for her. "As I walked in the court room, peace filled my heart," she says today. "I knew that even if I was found guilty, God would take care of me and His will would be done. Even though my future was in jeopardy, I was able to trust Him with the outcome."

On the second day of her trial, Karen was to hear her verdict. She knew the county had declared her guilty. Seeing Deputy Simpson caused her to start shaking. The facts he reported under oath were not the same as those she had given. Karen could only hope the jury would believe her.

The verdict came late in the afternoon. The jurors walked in the courtroom and wouldn't look at her. Karen tried to stay calm and not lose hope. Then, as she heard the words "Not guilty," relief filled her. She knew her life wasn't really in the hands of the jurors. God was her Counselor and Advocate.

As Karen left the courtroom, one of the pro-choice jurors looked into her eyes, smiled, and winked. Tears flowed down Karen's face. She knew justice was served but also that God had pierced the heart of a woman who was against what Karen believed. It was all worth it.

I eagerly expect and hope that I will in no way be ashamed, but will have sufficient courage so that now as always Christ will be exalted in my body, whether by life or by death.

(Philippians 1:20)

WEEK FIVE JOURNAL

—◦•◦—

⊨ On a scale of one to ten, how secure do you feel about what others are thinking of you?

⊨ How might your life be different if you could focus more on what God says is true about you?

⊨ What do you feel you need to do in order to be more acceptable to God?

⊨ Have you reached a place where you know and experience His love for you, regardless of what you do?

⊨ What Bible verse or passage of Scripture has been most meaningful to you this week? Why?

dawn delp
BETWEEN TWO ENEMIES

When Dawn Delp was twenty years old, she began praying for Kashmir, India, an area barely touched by the gospel. Every day, she pled with Jesus for this place she'd only read about that was desperate for the light of Jesus. She couldn't explain why God laid this geographical area on her heart, but she continued to pray. One day the Lord told her, "You will go and see that land someday."

Two years later, in the summer of 1998, her church decided to take a trip to that very place. Dawn and three other college students arrived in Kashmir. Heat and the smell of curry, human sweat, and roaming cows confronted her. In a land so foreign to her own, Dawn prayed.

Their small team met up with Indian Christians who were doctors. They decided to travel by car to several villages and treat the ill, setting up makeshift medical clinics. They also wanted to spend time encouraging existing missionaries and taking prayer walks—circling each town by foot praying for God to move in the hearts of the villagers. They wanted to reach the people by meeting their many physical needs and by ministering to their spiritual ones.

The fact that their team was small proved to be a great advantage because of the dangerous area they targeted. Residual fighting continued in that particular region, the result of a thirty-year war. By day, roads were relatively safe, but by nightfall, warfare raged between Pakistani and Indian factions. One day, as they traveled a road notorious for its evening skirmishes, a mudslide blocked their path, delaying their trip by several hours. They had hoped to reach their new base town during the day, but the delay prevented a timely arrival.

While they waited for debris to be cleared from the road, Dawn's team pulled out guitars and started singing. A crowd formed around them while an Indian doctor shared Jesus. He did this boldly, knowing that within a few hours all the listeners would be scattered and the police would not be able to track down each one. To share Christ in this unstable region was to risk imprisonment and possibly torture.

Two young men approached the doctor while he shared. They asked him spiritual questions. Later, they asked the doctor for Bibles.

Farther down the road, a collapsed bridge further postponed the missionaries' journey. Although thankful they weren't on the bridge at the time of the mayhem, they found themselves stranded at a tiny village. The villagers put up tents for the weary travelers.

The next day, tired from sleeping in makeshift tents and worrying about gunfire, the missionaries continued their journey on a narrow dirt road—just wide enough for one car. The road wound tortuously around a mountain pass, the car hugging the mountain's steep slope on one side and teasing the other edge, with a sheer drop one thousand feet to a river gorge below. The road had no guardrails, nothing to prevent cars from plummeting to the river below. Dawn prayed they'd meet any oncoming traffic—usually large buses and freight trucks—on straight parts of the road rather than curves. To calm themselves on the harrowing ride, the team members sang praise songs.

They passed a road sign that ordered travelers to stay off that road during certain hours, due to fighting. Dawn checked her watch. They were on the road within that very timeframe. She looked out the window to see Indian soldiers standing on the mountainside holding automatic weapons. Beyond the river gorge, Pakistani soldiers did the same, silently saluting the travelers with weapons at the ready. Dusk and then evening settled in. They could hear gunshots punctuating their drive.

Their driver, keenly aware of the danger of being sandwiched between two fighting factions, moved forward as quickly as he could. He took the corners too fast, spewing gravel and dirt behind them. The car jolted back and forth, leaning dangerously close to the gorge at one moment, the side mirror grazing the mountain's edge the next. Dawn's stomach rollicked as she sang—louder and louder—about God's deliverance, His goodness, His provision, His protection.

The team's singing intensified with every blind curve, with every approaching vehicle, with every *rat-tat-tat* of machine-gun fire. During this harrowing time, it struck Dawn that not only were they praising God in the midst of a fearful journey, but they were exalting Him in a region of great spiritual darkness. She smiled as she sang about the God who made the Indians and the Pakistanis, both of whom were lost in the darkness.

In the midst of that topsy-turvy journey, God gave Dawn peace. "I realized He was worthy of my life, no matter what the outcome," she says. "We were being obedient to His call to go, so we trusted He would take care of us."

The team reached its destination and checked into a hotel. Although they were fairly safe, gunfire rattled in the distance as they tried to sleep. The next day, they read a local paper that detailed the number of casualties on the road the previous evening. Later, when they recounted their adventure to a fellow missionary, she said, "Our driver had to turn off his headlights one evening on that road so we wouldn't be a target for the Pakistanis."

Near the end of her trip, Dawn and her teammates trekked ten thousand feet up the same mountains where they had seen the Indian soldiers holding their guns. The trip took five hot days. She prayed for the region, encouraging missionaries she met along the way. They treated the sick. The team took several prayer walks around the area, begging God to bring light to that spiritually dark place.

During that excursion, the mountains as a backdrop, Dawn asked the Lord what He wanted her to do with her life. From the mountain He told her, "Teach in a Muslim country, and serve long-term missionaries."

Today, she is doing just that—in Turkey, a Muslim country. She met her husband there. Together, they walk a new adventure, not so much on dusty, cliff-edged roads, but through the avenues of people's lives. The danger is still there, but God continues to give Dawn peace.

Let us not become weary in doing good, for at the proper time we will reap a harvest if we do not give up.

(Galatians 6:9)

gina waegele
CHILD OF GOD

From the outside, Gina Waegele looked as if she had her life together. Majoring in television news and video communication, she worked for Colorado State University's TV station, winning an Emmy Award for best student informational program and an award from the National College Broadcast Association for best newscast. Gina was beautiful, ambitious, and talented, and she soon anchored the newscasts for a small town's network affiliate as well as competed in beauty pageants. At twenty-one, she appeared to be on the fast track for a glamorous career.

Yet below the surface, memories haunted Gina. Her father had died suddenly when she was only thirteen, setting off a downward spiral of relationships in Gina's life and the lives of those she loved.

As a teenager, Gina suffered as she watched her older sister Christine's marriage end in a painful divorce. Christine was Gina's mentor and friend, and even though the sisters lived in different states, they shared an unusually close relationship. When Christine met and married her second husband, Gina celebrated with her. There was no hint that anything was wrong. Yet just six months after the wedding Christine was dead, the victim of domestic violence. Her husband strangled her to get her life-insurance money.

Still reeling from the loss of her sister, Gina entered college and found herself in a series of her own unhealthy relationships. Just months after Christine's death, Gina's possessive, controlling boyfriend beat her so badly that she wound up in the hospital. Recognizing the danger she was in, Gina cut ties with that boyfriend, only to fall into other hurtful relationships.

Her dating problems and an unresolved anger toward her sister's murderer forced Gina into a deep depression even as she received multiple broadcasting awards and recognition. By her senior year of college, Gina knew something had to change drastically. She couldn't keep living with the bitterness and pain that filled her heart.

Although Gina was raised in a Christian home and attended church as a child, she did not have a personal understanding of what it meant to live for Christ. In her heart, she thought that because she was making bad choices and not living the way a Christian should, God could never love her or forgive her. But when Gina reached the end of her own strength and her depression made her question whether she wanted to live or die, she finally cried out to God. "Show me that You're there. Show me that You're real!" she begged one night.

God did not answer her with a flash of light or an audible voice, but not long after that night, Gina felt a gentle tugging in her heart to find Christian roommates. She didn't know it yet, but God was working in her life.

Gina moved in with a few strong Christian friends, and they invited her to church. Still not sure what God was doing, she agreed to go. One service changed her life. Gina felt as if everything that happened that night, from the music to the message about the forgiveness of God, was written specifically for her.

Gina's struggle with bitterness, especially toward the man who had killed her sister, had been eating at her. She cried herself to sleep at night and lost her temper over the smallest things. Deeply rooted anger controlled Gina's life, making it impossible for her to understand forgiveness, especially the forgiveness of God.

Yet Gina felt God whisper to her heart, "You have to forgive him." She struggled against the idea. How could anyone ask her to do that, after what the man did to her family? But God was persistent, and finally Gina understood how her anger and hate consumed her. She began to pray, and slowly the bitterness faded and she was able to let go and truly forgive. Not only did Gina find peace from the tragedy, but she also caught a clear glimpse of God's forgiveness. If she, a flawed human being, could forgive someone who hurt her and the people around her so much, the Creator of the universe could obviously find forgiveness for the things she had done. After so many years, Gina finally understood the message of the Cross, and it changed her whole life.

A few months after Gina recommitted her life to God, she faced another challenge of faith. She competed in the 1997 Miss Colorado pageant and won the title of First Runner-Up. It was a great honor—Gina had never placed in the top five in any pageant—but it was only the beginning. Six months after the contest, the pageant board of directors took the crown away from the reigning Miss Colorado and called on Gina to serve out the rest of the year. Gina accepted the responsibility. Acting as Miss Colorado gave her the opportunity to travel across the state and talk about her platform issue—domestic violence awareness—and share her own story.

Life as the new Miss Colorado wasn't easy. The original pageant winner sued to get her title back, and the media constantly pulled Gina into the controversy, often trying to portray her as the villain. Two weeks before Gina's term would have ended, the court sided in favor of the original pageant winner and instructed Gina to give the title and responsibilities back. As quickly as it started, her reign as Miss Colorado ended.

God had a plan for this as well. In her final press conference, Gina was asked if she would try to sue for the title. Looking calm and confident, Gina answered, "My identity is not in a crown; it's not in a car; it's not in money; and it's not in the title of Miss Colorado. My identity is in my faith in God." In that moment, Gina realized the full impact of her statement. She was indeed a child of God, and that was more important than anything else she would do or anyone she would date. It was not important whether she was someone's girlfriend or a TV star.

Gina considered this new perspective carefully as she considered what to do next in her life. After she graduated college, she made a radical decision to leave her job in television and dedicate her life to helping young people develop healthy relationships centered in Christ.

Gina turned down high-paying corporate jobs, choosing instead to work with a small nonprofit organization called Friends First. As the national program director, Gina travels across the country, speaking to high-school students in public and private schools about abstinence and healthy dating relationships. She continues to share her story, with all of its highs and lows, and whenever she can, she includes her favorite Bible verses, James 1:2–4: "Consider it pure joy, my brothers, whenever you face trials of many kinds, because you know that the testing of your faith develops perseverance. Perseverance must finish its work so that you may be mature and complete, not lacking anything."

Although Gina wasn't always sure how to pay her bills in the beginning, God always provided for her needs, showing her over and over again that this was the ministry He called her to from the beginning. All of her struggles, all of her experiences have led her to where she is today, where she can speak confidently about who she is, and who we all are, as children of God.

For it is by grace you have been saved, through faith—and this not from yourselves, it is the gift of God—not by works, so that no one can boast.

(Ephesians 2:8–9)

dana

FROM DEATH TO LIFE

D ana learned early of God's love for her and never doubted that He was real. In her simple understanding, He was her friend. Dana continued to grow in her trust in Him and His extravagant love. On her ninth birthday she made it official and went to the altar, asking Him to be her Lord.

The crossroads of her existence came when at twenty-five years old she felt God ask if she'd be willing to move across the world to care for little children in Africa. She had doubts. But she felt so full of His love, she couldn't imagine keeping it to herself. After lots of prayer, her answer was a resounding yes! It was a decision that would uproot all Dana knew about God.

After many hours of travel, the young woman arrived in Mozambique, a country located on the dry, dusty, eastern border of Africa. Dana's new home was in an orphanage, which housed at that time approximately four hundred children, most of them abandoned, some deathly ill, and all broken and hurting. A wild mix of intense emotions arrived with Dana, but she had ministered in some pretty rough areas of other countries and in inner-city situations, so she was confident God had adequately prepared her to handle that too.

Dana adored the dark-skinned people of Mozambique, soon loving them as if she'd grown up with their soil under her feet. Otencia, a little girl eight years old, was one of Dana's shadows at the orphanage. She visited Dana daily, sometimes bringing bread and tea in the morning for breakfast. Each week she insisted on helping Dana hand-wash her clothes and sweep her room. Dana couldn't believe how responsible she was for one so young.

The conditions were shocking, but Dana's faith was sure. God wanted to demonstrate His love and care to those children. She and her team had many trials to overcome, one being that Dana became very ill with malaria, a disease passed through mosquitoes. Still, she considered that merely a part of the sacrifice—a cross she would gladly bear for Jesus.

A few months after Dana's arrival, an outbreak of cholera, a very deadly disease from contaminated water, hit her orphanage. For almost two weeks, Dana spent days and nights transporting the children who were most ill to a tent hospital. There, under the tattered canvas, she lay them on rough wooden tables, the only hospital "beds" available. Each trip, Dana saw them getting worse, not better. All she could do was watch as the life drained out of several of those precious ones, their bodies growing limp, their breathing slowing, their skin cooling. It was actually a tent of death, and each visit there dented Dana's faith a little more. But she held on, doing what needed to be done.

Then Otencia became ill. It was cholera, and as her energy and strength faded, Dana faced the unthinkable task. It was part of her service, part of her mission, so she carried the young girl through the night, Otencia's soft face held to Dana's, mixing their tears all the way to the tent.

Dana tried to speak words of comfort, but could Otencia understand? Leaving her there with those fawn eyes looking back at her—eyes filled with fear when Dana peeled Otencia's hands from her arms, leaving her to lie on the table. Dana turned and walked away. Would Otencia make it? She could only hope.

But as Otencia's cries faded into the darkness behind Dana, she found there was no hope left inside. Her soul collapsed in on itself, sucking what was left of her heart into a dark hole of doubt and questions about the goodness of God in the face of such anguish.

Back at the orphanage, death continued to take others. Apart from the cholera epidemic, AIDS, pneumonia, and untreated disease had claimed three more lives. The team had to continue on, but Dana cried day and night, "Where are You in the midst of this, God?" She endured weeks of questioning and bitterness against this God whom she had loved and trusted since she was a little girl. *How can I ever trust Him again?*

For weeks, the Lord remained silent. No answers came. No comfort was given. And then, in the middle of a worship service for the missionaries, He broke the silence in clear, unmistakable terms. Dana was down on her knees, on the concrete floor, when one of the leaders began to read from John 12:24: "Unless a kernel of wheat falls to the ground and dies, it remains only a single seed. But if it dies, it produces many seeds."

As she heard these words, Dana felt her spirit began to groan deep within her. Before she knew exactly what was happening, she had fallen on her face and was crying out, "Kill

Me! God, just kill me!" Dana was dying. She was dying to all that she had known before and all that she thought God was . . . and wasn't. Dying to her need to know why; dying a beautiful, hard death. And in exchange for Dana's death, the Lord breathed into her new life—and with this life came these words: "Dana, My goodness is never determined by your circumstances."

In the midst of all the darkness, a new light of understanding began to grow. God's goodness is one of those absolutes in this world of suffering. It is goodness that passes beyond all suffering, all death, and all brokenness. In His goodness, there in Mozambique, He brought Dana into a death of her own.

She realized that somewhere along the way, she had become convinced that the Lord was only as good as the events in her life. When life was all right, God seemed loving and close. When things felt as if they were crashing down around her, Dana questioned His motives, forgetting that He was the one who never changed. That's why she had to die. Dana had to die to herself and all her expectations, so she could see Him for who He really was.

And as Dana died, she began to live in a new way, letting the Lord show her His heart even in the midst of such a distorted and painful world. He showed her that while suffering and death had so overwhelmed her, it was His goodness that met those precious little ones at the gates of eternity. It was His voice that ushered them into the land of eternal living— free from the bondage of earth. It was His perfect love that kept many more from death and suffering during those critical days and weeks.

It was certainly His goodness that brought Dana to a place of spiritual death, she saw, allowing her to be raised to new life in Him. Heaven now fills her thoughts. She says, "How can I describe the abundant life waiting for us who are willing to die to ourselves and find real life hidden with Christ in God?"

Dana is willing to work and believe.

Let heaven fill your thoughts. Do not think only about things down here on earth. For you died when Christ died, and your real life is hidden with Christ in God.

(Colossians 3:2–3 NLT)

Mary

MOTHER OF GOD

How brave am I? Can I bear this call on my life without breaking? Why have I been chosen to mother the Son of God? I'm only thirteen—how can this be true? I'm a virgin!

Her story began with a troubling visitation. Mary, a young Jewish girl living in Nazareth, heard the call of God—and not at the most convenient of times. She was engaged to a man named Joseph from King David's lineage. Then an angel appeared and said, "Greetings, you who are highly favored! The Lord is with you." Mary, understandably, was frightened and "greatly troubled" (Luke 1:28–29). But the angel assured her she had nothing to fear.

Mary, you have found favor with God. You will be with child and give birth to a son, and you are to give him the name Jesus. He will be great and will be called the Son of the Most High. The Lord God will give him the throne of his father David, and he will reign over the house of Jacob forever; his kingdom will never end. (Luke 1:30–33)

Mary responded, "I am the Lord's servant. I'll do it! I will submit to His will for me."

Not surprisingly, after Mary said yes to God, her life changed dramatically. When the angel had approached her, he didn't explain everything but simply heard her submission to God. So God's plan went forward, and Mary, barely in her teens and a peasant, carried in her body part of the Trinity.

The months ahead were not easy. Joseph didn't believe Mary's story at first. She couldn't blame him—it was almost too fantastical to imagine. And the couple lived at a time when women were stoned for adultery. Joseph planned to divorce Mary quietly, which would spare her life. But then God sent an angel to Joseph in a dream, explaining that Mary was indeed carrying the Messiah. The angel told him that His name should be Jesus, because He would save all people from their sins. So then the young couple carried the burden together. The Lord knew they would need each other in the days to come.

During the pregnancy, Caesar Augustus issued a decree for a census to be taken of the entire Roman world. Mary and Joseph had to travel from Nazareth in Galilee to Judea, to Bethlehem, the town of David, because they belonged to David's lineage. It was about a three-day trip, and Mary knew the baby was coming soon—but not exactly how soon.

While the couple stayed in Bethlehem, Jesus was born. This wasn't exactly a dream birth. No rooms were available for the couple at the inn, and Joseph could locate as shelter only a stable. There, on a bed of hay, their son was born. Mary wrapped Jesus in strips of cloth to keep Him warm and still. Despite His humble beginning, the baby radiated God's glory. Joseph and Mary couldn't take their eyes off Him.

Mary kept blinking through tears to see Him more clearly. She couldn't believe she was finally holding her son—God's Son, the Savior of the world. Her arms trembled as she cuddled Him, and she felt a joy she had never known before.

Soon shepherds, whom angels had told about the young couple, arrived. They were just as amazed as Mary and Joseph. In that quiet, lonely night, Joseph, Jesus, and Mary found comfort in the company of shepherds and some friendly barn animals.

Those early moments of Jesus' life were precious to Mary. She held Him tightly all night, pondering what the Lord had done to bring about the miracle. It seemed so—impossible. What if she had said no to God's plan? In the silence broken only by the quiet breathing of sleeping animals, Mary rejoiced. All fear and anxiety left her heart.

Soon after Jesus' birth, the Magi from the East came to worship Him. Herod, the ruthless king, was very disturbed by this. He had murdered his wife and three sons, and in his rage, he gave orders to kill all the boys in Bethlehem, hoping to destroy Mary's son. But Joseph had another visitation from an angel, who said, "Take the child and his mother and escape to Egypt. Stay there until I tell you, for Herod is going to search for the child and kill him" (Luke 2:13). The little family stayed in Egypt until they heard of Herod's death.

Through all these trials, the Lord's faithfulness protected Mary. He accomplished all He promised through her. Yet as she raised her son Jesus, she still often wondered, *Why me? Surely there were other, older, more qualified women who could have taken on the task.* Yet, in God's wisdom, He chose Mary. As scandalous as the plan seemed at the time, she knew His way had to be the best. She had to trust Him.

Mary's story continues to cause people to question why God picked such an unconventional way to save the world. Why a thirteen-year-old girl? And Joseph's anguish and shame—couldn't Jesus have been born under more favorable, conventional circumstances? Why couldn't the inn have had room to house the young couple when they most needed it? Why was Herod reigning at the time—a man who thought nothing of killing babies? So many mothers' hearts were broken.

No doubt God could have chosen an easier road for Mary, but then she—and we—would have never known emphatically that "nothing is impossible with God" (Luke 1:37).

My soul glorifies the Lord
*   and my spirit rejoices in God my Savior,*
for he has been mindful
*   of the humble state of his servant.*
From now on all generations
*   will call me blessed,*
for the Mighty One has done great things for me—
*   holy is this name.*
His mercy extends to those who fear him,
*   from generation to generation.*

(Luke 1:46–50)

---

bethany
PART OF THE FAMILY

When Bethany was a senior in high school, her English teacher assigned each student a book of the Bible to examine for literary allusions and parallels. Bethany remembers digging an old, dusty Bible out of a box in the basement and reading Ruth's promise to her mother-in-law, Naomi: "Your people will be my people and your God my God" (Ruth 1:16).

Abused and abandoned by her biological father and struggling in her relationship with her stepfather, Bethany read the words sadly. They described a sense of belonging she had never felt and couldn't imagine experiencing.

Bethany had almost forgotten about her English class assignment a few months later when she moved to a nearby city to begin college. A girl in her dorm invited Bethany to a church worship service, and she agreed to go.

That night, as the band played praise songs, Bethany found what she was missing: the unconditional love of a Father. By the second song, she was sobbing. "I wanted everything that I saw there that night," she says. "So I asked Jesus into my life.

And for a few moments it was pure bliss; I got a glimpse of eternity."

And then, she says, life went downhill.

When Bethany told her parents that she had joined a church and a Bible study, they were suspicious, then hostile. While she was growing up, they had encouraged her to explore as many different faiths as she wanted. But once she chose one—Christianity—their support disappeared. Bethany's stepfather had been raised in a Christian church, but he had turned away from it. He convinced Bethany's mother, a non-practicing Catholic, that her daughter was being brainwashed. Bethany repeatedly invited her parents to attend her church themselves, but they never did.

Bethany's faith blossomed during her year at school, while she was surrounded by caring Christian friends and a loving church family. But when she went back to her rural hometown for the summer, her relationship with her parents went from bad to worse. They forbade her to contact her church friends, her boyfriend, or his missionary family, and they constantly attacked her faith. When her mother found Bethany reading her Bible one afternoon, she took it away. "There are better ways for you to spend your time. Don't let me catch you reading this again," she snapped. Her parents even took away a ring with a cross on it that Bethany wore.

Her mother and stepfather were convinced that Bethany had joined a cult and when she disagreed, they accused her of not "honoring" her parents. They told her over and over that she was "fragile," a follower who too easily believed what she was told. Perhaps that was true of the old Bethany, who had been quiet and compliant with her authoritarian stepfather's will. But the new Bethany had discovered the unconditional love of Christ, and she wasn't about to give it up.

Without intending to, Bethany upset her parents even more when she decided to major in international studies and one day become a missionary. "They told me that I was failing," she says. "I think they were really disappointed that I wasn't going to be a doctor as I had hoped, or a lawyer as I had talked about."

Sensing that they were losing control of their daughter, Bethany's mother and stepfather refused to let her return to college the following quarter. They said that since she was not good at making her own decisions at age nineteen, they would begin making them for her again.

But her parents underestimated Bethany's new faith and the determination that a heavenly Father had given her. After praying and agonizing for weeks, she decided she needed to move out. "I couldn't handle being so cut off from God and from fellowship. I was such a new Christian that I was aching for more support, for more of a community. I wanted my church, I wanted my prayer partners, I wanted God," she says sadly.

Bethany made arrangements to move back to her college town and live with a young married couple, even if she couldn't enroll that quarter. While her parents didn't say much when Bethany announced her plans to move, it was clear the healing Bethany hoped for was still a long way away.

Not long after she moved, Bethany applied to Youth With a Mission's Discipleship Training School in Switzerland. The six-month program of study and ministry seemed like just what she needed to grow in her faith.

Bethany's plans upset her parents. They saw overseas study as another sign of their daughter's "cult" involvement, and they did everything they could to prevent her leaving. They refused to hand over her passport. Claiming she was mentally unstable, they threatened to have her committed to a mental institution. They tried to cancel her airline reservations. Over and over, they told Bethany that she was not smart enough, not responsible enough, not strong enough to make her own decisions. But Bethany knew that God was calling her to the program. And so she went.

Even in Switzerland, Bethany's faith was tested by her family. Her mother, who had suffered from depression for years, became suicidal. She called Bethany to announce that their strained relationship was what made her want to kill herself. She called another time to say that she had left a letter with Bethany's aunt "in case I'm not here when you get back."

Bethany was devastated. "There was a little prayer attic where we were staying, and I spent so many hours up there asking God, 'Why are You still allowing this?' I went back and forth between being angry and knowing that I had to trust Him. I prayed, 'If there is something to learn, show it to me, and I can keep pressing through this.'"

From Switzerland, Bethany's mission team went to Morocco. There they worked in schools and missionary programs, teaching English and helping wherever they were needed. It was there, essentially cut off from her family, that Bethany began to see what she had been learning through her conflict.

"I think God taught me grace and compassion," she says. "In Morocco, I realized how much I want the girls around me to know that they are loved. Even if no one else shows them that, they will at least know it from me. Morocco is a very patriarchal society, and a lot of the girls I met were ruled by their fathers. I think I helped them because I identified with them. I knew what it was like to grow up feeling as if you didn't have a dad, or knowing that he was there but you could never connect with him. I could share what I had learned—that God accepts us into *His* family."

Now home, Bethany is on fire for God and excited about the work she feels called to do. She misses her family, who have now cut her off completely, but she knows that she is being obedient to God as she continues to prepare for a career as a missionary. She clings to the words of Ruth, who was also torn between family loyalty and the will of God when she made her promise to Naomi.

"I think there is hope in any situation," Bethany says confidently. "I have talked to people whose family situations are similar. [Reconciliation] could take seven years. It could take twenty. But God allows us to walk through hard times so that we can follow Him, and He can be a beacon. And I remind myself that even if my parents are disowning me, I still belong to His family."

In love, he predestined us to be adopted as his sons through Jesus Christ, in accordance with his pleasure and will—to the praise of his glorious grace.

(Ephesians 1:4–6)

WEEK SIX JOURNAL

+= Does your view of God's goodness change with your circumstances?

+= What kinds of things make you question Him the most?

+= What "why" questions do you wrestle with the most?

+= What would happen if you "died" to the need for answers and let Him fill you with a new kind of trust in His goodness?

+= What Bible verse or passage of Scripture has been most meaningful to you this week? Why?

jennifer mckinnon
ALONE AT THE PODIUM

The graduation audience sat quietly as Jennifer McKinnon turned away from the podium and placed her notes beside her folding chair. As she began to sit down, the audience stood, a cheer erupting from the filled-to-capacity high-school stadium. Jennifer smiled. And she thanked God for the greatest evangelism opportunity of her young life.

Jennifer had met Jesus when she was five. The leaders in children's church shared the gospel with Jennifer and her friends. She knew, even then, that she needed Jesus.

She continued to attend church, but it wasn't until high school that she started serving Him with all her heart. For three years, she led a weekly Bible study before school, interacting with all kinds of students. She ran cross-country, so she befriended the athletes in her school. She was president of the band, so she made friends with other musicians. Her desire was to share the love of Jesus with anyone in her school, regardless of his or her position or interests.

"I saw God do great things in the lives of other students," she says. "I tried to show people that being a Christian isn't about being a radical for rules but about being a radical for love."

Jennifer wasn't part of the "in" crowd when she entered high school. Still, she spent her time embracing all sorts of students, sharing the love she'd come to know. "I wasn't a cheerleader or the quarterback's girlfriend," she says. "But at the end of my senior year, I was voted Best All Around by my peers. This wasn't because I was popular or pretty or smart. I pray it was because I took time to love people as Christ loves people."

By her senior year, Jennifer felt a keen sense of urgency regarding her classmates. She knew her graduation speech was her last chance to share the gospel with them.

Only one person knew the content of her valedictory speech before she gave it. Not even her parents knew what she was going to say. She was supposed to rehearse the speech in front of her English teacher for approval, but she knew if she did that, she wouldn't be allowed to give it. Earlier in the school year, that teacher had quipped, "Jennifer will never amount to anything because she's too concerned with family and religion." In class, this teacher berated her for her beliefs and intentionally asked jarring and antagonizing questions.

It was an unlikely place to find persecution—in Nederland, Texas, a small town near the Louisiana border. But instead of discouraging her, the teacher's criticism made Jennifer all the more passionate about sharing Christ, particularly when she stood in front of her peers on graduation night.

The salutatorian rehearsed his speech for the English teacher, a speech full of platitudes such as "Let us give thanks to a higher power, whoever that may be—Allah, Buddha, God." When Jennifer rehearsed, she gave an alternative speech. She worried she'd be in trouble for doing that, so she submitted the entire manuscript to another teacher who did not hold her in disdain. That teacher approved.

Jennifer wanted her speech to be different—something that touched people and clearly communicated the gospel. She felt God had given her this final opportunity to share Him, as if her speech were an exclamation point to a life lived for Christ in high school. She claimed the words of Jeremiah as her own: "Then the LORD stretched out His hand and touched my mouth, and the LORD said to me, / 'Behold, I have put My words in your mouth'" (1:9 NASB).

She spoke about her grandfather, a sharecropper, who had no education beyond elementary school. She described him as a brilliant craftsman. "Education doesn't make you a success," she said. "Having a purpose does."

Standing in front of thousands of friends and family and community members, she took a breath. "If I could leave you with a message, it would be this: thank God for the blessings He's given you, and live your life for Him."

She ended her speech by singing "How Could I Ask for More," a song written by Christian recording artist Cindy Morgan. When she finished the crowd was silent—until the moment she turned to see the town standing, clapping, and hollering its approval.

It just so happened that she had to pick up her diploma from the teacher who was supposed to approve her speech. Jennifer walked into the classroom and waited.

"Interesting speech." The teacher handed her the diploma.

"Thank you," Jennifer said. "God gave it to me." She left the room smiling—knowing that God had given her words to speak, lives to touch.

Jennifer knew God was calling her into a life of full-time ministry even then. "Most people thought this meant I was going to marry a pastor, but I knew in my heart God was calling *me* to ministry. It wasn't about the person I would marry. It was about what God wanted to do with my life."

God continued to put words in Jennifer's mouth, providing many opportunities to speak in college and beyond. He burned in her a deep desire to teach His truth to teenage girls. "This led me to cofound SAGE Girls Ministries while I was in college," she recounts. Started with a little bit of change kept in a pickle jar, SAGE Ministries now reaches across the United States with the message that it's never too early to begin serving Jesus Christ. Its mission statement reads: "To equip a new generation with the resources to develop virtuous character through intimate worship and the sharing of personal testimonies and biblical truths in a relevant, God-honoring manner."

The heartbeat of SAGE Ministries is to reach, teach, and train young women to impact their communities and the world. "As a high school student," Jennifer says, "I realized and witnessed firsthand that God could use me if I was willing. I want other girls to realize this same truth—that ministry doesn't have to begin when you're thirty or forty. They are not merely the future of the church—they are also the present church. I want to tell young girls that it's time to stand up and make a difference today for the kingdom of Christ."

Jennifer continues to be passionate about expanding the kingdom of Christ, traveling to Germany and Russia and sharing Him in places where people's hearts are calloused to the truth. "In both places I have felt His presence very near as I witnessed in His name," she says.

But it all started on a lonely platform in front of a silent audience where Jennifer dared to believe God would put His words in her mouth.

———•———— ————•———— ————•———— ————•———— ————•———— ————•——

Let your light shine before men, that they may see your good deeds and praise your Father in heaven.

(Matthew 5:16)

———•———— ————•———— ————•———— ————•———— ————•———— ————•——

britany miller
REVIVAL BIBLE STUDY

Britany Miller met Jesus in the Waffle House parking lot when she was four years old. "How does someone get saved?" she asked her parents. They led her through the steps to salvation. Eleven years later, she met Jesus afresh, this time as a Bridegroom who took great delight in her.

She remembers her encounter with Jesus as if it were a movie playing on the screen of her mind. Nearly a sophomore in high school, she had become self-conscious, longing for everyone's approval. Because of this, she placed herself in compromising situations and was drifting away from Jesus.

One day, on a grassy, green hill as a summer evening breeze washed over her, Britany wrote her first love letter to Jesus as the sun tucked itself in for the night. "During that weekend with Jesus, I experienced love and attention that for once looked at my inner beauty, and in the midst of my shamefulness called me beautiful."

The next summer, before Britany's junior year of high school, the Lord spoke to her. He said, "I want you to start a small-group Bible study for girls."

She agreed. The first week of August, she started with three girls from her school in attendance. There was nothing like that going on in her school, so she knew she was taking a leap of faith. One month later, the three girls turned into thirty. She called the group Spoken For to show they were committed to their faith. Soon after, another friend decided to start something similar for guys. In January of that school year, the two groups decided to meet jointly once a month, calling that meeting CoEd.

Sheltered in Britany's basement, seventy kids came to the first CoEd event. Thirty asked Jesus to be the Lord of their lives. None of the kids who came were churched kids—they were the band members, druggies, and popular students who roamed the halls of Britany's high school. Fifteen-year-old Britany was surprised to see so many kids from such a broad spectrum come to faith in Jesus Christ.

Britany, who attends Roswell Church of God in Woodstock, Georgia, credits Mark and Gwenn, her youth leaders, for mentoring her while she leads Spoken For. It was Gwenn who first helped Britany see herself as a bride of Christ, as His princess.

Though she's involved in many aspects of school, including being captain of the cheerleading squad, Britany chooses to spend most of her time planning retreats, preparing to speak, praying for friends—all things related to Spoken For. Because of that, "I feel as if I am out on a limb for Him every day," she says. "What is Christianity if we don't venture out to a place where we have to have a little faith? Every time I speak, do a retreat, hand out flyers for Spoken For, go on a mission trip, or pray passionately for someone, I am making myself vulnerable."

Every Tuesday night, when Spoken For meets, Britany has learned to wait on God for what He wants her to say. "Each week I prepare a message," she says. "This is all in faith that the girls are going to be there. There have been times I was to speak at a church or retreat and the Lord told me simply 'Go without a message.' I had to have faith that when I opened my mouth, He would give me the words to say."

More than learning how to trust God for messages, Britany relishes spending time with Jesus. She loves to enter His presence while singing or listening to praise and worship music. "This is the place where He searches me and either heals me or breaks me, depending on what I need." As a busy student leading a new ministry, she's needed refreshment from the Lord. "These are the moments that give me the strength to carry on this ministry for the last two years. These are the times He has whispered to me exactly what the girls needed to hear."

She likens herself to Esther—available to others in "such a time as this" (Esther 4:14). "The biggest lesson the Lord has taught me is that His people are desperate. His eyes wander the earth, looking for someone to step forth, to not remain silent, to be an Esther for this generation."

She still marvels that God chose to save and use her for His purposes at Woodstock High School, located in a suburban community thirty minutes north of Atlanta. "The Lord spared me," she says. "He gave me beauty for ashes and called me out to go forth and allow Him to use me."

More than sixty kids from Britany's high school have met Jesus Christ because of the ministry she started out of simple obedience. Weekly, girls approach her for prayer and advice. "I've had girls admit to drug use, suicide attempts, molestation, sexual promiscuity, pregnancy, alcoholism—you name it. And they have all come to me during a Spoken For meeting and looked for godly counsel. I know nothing, but I do serve a God who knows everything. He has spoken through me to these hurting girls."

Britany loves sharing Jesus with the friends she meets through Spoken For. "This has been fairly easy for me, sharing Jesus with these girls. They are hungry and God is willing to give them food. He just needs someone to deliver it for Him. It's not that He is looking for anybody perfect or incredible, just a willing person. With a simple okay on my part, the Lord overflows my life with more blessing than I can hold, and a plan I can't even comprehend."

Britany is now on the cusp of a new life at Lee University. She has a dream: she wants to start a new ministry to high school and college-age girls while she's there. In the midst of school, cheerleading, and ministry, Britany realizes that only Jesus matters. "For this ministry to be successful, I have to go beyond people, beyond the physical, and enter into a supernatural place where I see with spiritual eyes and ears. I am not satisfied with a glance or one word from Him."

She's found life in ministry lonely at times. "Of course everyone sees me preaching every Tuesday, but what does God see? What does He require? These are the secret decisions I have to make on my own in order for God's blessing and favor to be upon us. Everyone wants to be there when things are easy, but when it's hard, sometimes the Lord requires me to go forth alone."

In this place of willingness and even loneliness, Britany has been able to see God do miraculous things, including changing the lives of those around her. "When we allow ourselves to undergo a purification process and then are brave enough to speak the word of the Lord with genuine motives and a passionate heart, nothing is impossible."

At eighteen, Britany's had the privilege of seeing just that. Who knew what could come from a spiritual encounter in a Waffle House parking lot.

As obedient children, do not conform to the evil desires you had when you lived in ignorance. But, just as He who called you is holy, so be holy in all you do; for it is written: "Be holy, because I am holy."

(1 Peter 1:14–16)

---

shirley
THE JOY OF THE LORD

Meeting Shirley is a pleasant experience. Joy shines in her eyes and her beaming smile. She seems to know the secret to living with gratitude. She wears no banners of self-entitlement; she is unassuming and sweet. But behind her pleasant, jovial nature is a woman with strong faith who understands the pain of rejection and loneliness.

Shirley grew up without her mother and father. She was three when her mom died, and soon after her dad abandoned the family. Shirley then was sent to live with her aunt and uncle.

Life on the farm with her cousins and new guardians was not easy. Shirley remembers as a very young girl wanting desperately to fit into the family. She prayed, "God, please help me to be a better little girl so Aunt Edna and Uncle Chester will love me." Shirley worked hard around the farm but never received praise or a second glance for her hard work. *Maybe if I just scrub the floors harder or wash the dishes better, they will learn to like me,* she would think.

Edna and Chester did not treat Shirley the way they treated their own children. They often spanked her when a situation wasn't her fault. Her cousins never had to do any work, but Shirley worked from sunrise to bedtime each day. She had to wash her face and brush her teeth outside in the bitter cold. At such a young age, Shirley knew only a life of labor. The day was full of washing, cooking, and cleaning for the whole family and the hired hands, day in and day out. The workload never decreased, no matter how much faster she worked.

Once she asked, "Aunt Edna, can I go shopping with you today?"

"You can't go. You are too ugly," answered her aunt.

Despite Shirley's early experience with rejection, she knew the Lord loved her. Her favorite day of the week was Sunday. Her aunt and uncle did allow her to go to church with them, and how she loved it. There, Shirley learned songs and hymns of praise that sustained her through long days of drudgery: "I sing because I'm happy / I sing because I'm free / For His eye is on the sparrow, / And I know He watches me."

Singing became a healing balm for her soul. The barn became her sanctuary, where she sang to the cows and the pigs while she went about her chores. She knew God cared for the animals and for her. Though the days were long and she was always tired, she had strength to sing praises to the Lord, offering up her calloused hands and lonely heart to Him.

One Sunday, Shirley's aunt and uncle invited Pastor and Mrs. Johnson, a young African American couple, over after church. Shirley was instantly drawn to them. They paid attention to her. She could tell they even liked her. For the first time in her life, she felt love. Over time, they became the parents she never had; she called them Mom and Pop Johnson. Through the years they grew closer, and Mom and Pop became aware of how mistreated Shirley was. They kept an eye on her, even though they had eight children of their own.

It didn't matter how hard she tried, Shirley's life with her aunt and uncle never improved. Finally, at age sixteen, she decided to run away. Out on her own, she managed to get a job and support herself. On the weekends she stayed with Mom and Pop Johnson. She felt safe, loved, and accepted at their house—a part of the family. Mom and Pop even decided to name their youngest daughter after Shirley.

As Shirley grew older, she desired a family and home of her own. She married Robert when she was twenty-one, and the couple were very involved church members who sang at weddings, funerals, and revivals. Life was good, and with several children, Shirley was finally building the family and home she desired.

But after a while, Robert grew restless. One Sunday after church, he said, "Shirley, aren't you just sick and tired of going to church?" Shirley knew something was desperately wrong. Soon, Robert left the family.

Once again, Shirley endured the pain of rejection and loneliness, and she was left with a dairy farm to run. Shirley cried out to God for help. She wondered if Robert had left because she was so hard to love, and she asked God to show her if it was her fault. Robert did come back for a while, only to leave his family again.

Shirley had five children to take care of and didn't know how she could manage the farm. The cows needed to be milked, but she could not tend to her infant son and other children as well as run a farm. Soon, the owners picked up the cows; Shirley couldn't pay for them. The police found Robert, but he told the officials he had never been married and had no children. Robert was thrown into prison for a while, but Shirley purposely lost contact with him to protect the children.

In her deep despair, she began to wonder if even God loved her. Perhaps she deserved all that had happened to her. Providentially, in the midst of her doubting and questioning, Shirley opened her Bible to Exodus 33:

> Then Moses said . . . "How will anyone know that you are pleased with me and with your people unless you go with us? What else will distinguish me and your people from all the other people on the face of the earth?"
>
> And the LORD said to Moses, "I will do the very thing you have asked, because I am pleased with you and I know you by name. . . . I will cause all my goodness to pass in front of you, and I will proclaim my name. . . . I will have mercy on whom I will have mercy, and I will have compassion on whom I will have compassion." (vv. 15–17, 19)

Shirley knew God had opened her Bible to those verses to remind her that He loved her with a fierce love. In the midst of her sorrow and pain, God's care and mercy were there.

The days ahead were not easy. She began to feel nervous, living all alone on the dairy farm with her children, and decided to look for a better home. Shirley remembered a Christian family, the Buchsmans, that she had met a while ago; for some reason she thought they might help. Driving all night with her children to Colorado, she found their house. Miraculously, rather than turn her away, they said, "The Lord has already been talking to us, and we are supposed to take care of you and your children."

The next day, Shirley and her children moved in, ready to help manage the couple's farm, thankful for God's miraculous provision. The days began at 4:00 AM with daily devotions and milking the cows before the kids went to school. Shirley taught her children to sing in the barn, just as she had as a child. They knew their father had abandoned them but that the Lord was taking care of them.

There they stayed for three years, until the Buchsman family decided to sell the farm. Shirley knew God would provide another house. He was her family's Husband and Father, and he proved it when one day a complete stranger knocked at the door and said, "Shirley, I have a home for you." Without question, she knew the Lord was providing for their needs once again.

Throughout uncertain times, Shirley taught her children to sing, and there was laughter wherever they went together. Even as a single mom of five, Shirley was always able to provide a safe home for the family, something she never had as a child. And there was always an abundance of love for everyone.

No doubt, because of the loving home Shirley maintained, today all of her children are Christians. Her joy through the hard times made God's love a reality.

Faith is being sure of what we hope for and certain of what we do not see.

(Hebrews 11:1)

---

claire wibabara
THE MINISTRY OF RECONCILIATION

So many men had betrayed Claire, she vowed never to trust one again. It started in her childhood. Her family, ethnic Tutsis from Rwanda, fled the violence and discrimination of their troubled African homeland, moving to Burundi when Claire was a small child. But their dream of safety and happiness was short lived. Not long after the family settled into their new home, Claire's father abandoned his wife and children and ran away with another woman.

A lonely teenager, Claire longed for love, especially from a man. Instead, she faced more heartbreak and abuse. A schoolteacher raped her but was never punished for his crime. Claire turned to her boyfriend for comfort, but when she was seventeen she discovered she was pregnant, and he too left her.

Several years after her son was born, Claire left her child with her mother and sister and returned to Rwanda to find work and support her family. There she lived with an uncle.

Rwanda was a dangerous place in the early 1990s. Decades of conflict had built suspicion and hatred between the major ethnic groups, and violence simmered all of the time. Not long after Claire returned to her home country, a wave of anti-Tutsi riots broke out in the area where she was living. In the ensuing chaos, someone turned the young Tutsi woman over to the vicious Hutu army.

The army did not kill Claire; instead, officials accused her of being a spy for Burundi, which was often a base for Tutsi rebellions and guerilla attacks. They threw Claire in jail, beating and torturing her almost every day. She was not allowed to contact her family; no one knew where Claire was, or even whether she had lived through the riots.

Frightened and alone, Claire cried out to God from her dark prison cell. She was not a Christian, but she realized if there was a God, He was the only one who knew where she was. To her surprise, she heard a voice answer, "I love you. You will survive prison, and you will serve Me."

Claire knew that the voice was God's, but she was not sure if she could trust Him. The voice was a male one, and she had suffered so much already from males in her life. Would a God who spoke with the voice of a man really help her?

After two months in prison, Claire was finally released, only to face an even greater danger. In 1994, Rwanda's simmering volcano of ethnic tension erupted. Waves of extremist Hutu mobs, supported by members of the military and government, poured into the streets, intent on destroying the Tutsi people. In just one hundred days, machete and rifle-wielding extremist Hutus butchered as many as one million Tutsis and moderate Hutus, often executing them in their homes or on the street.

Every Rwandan was required to carry an identification card listing his or her ethnicity; that spring and summer, a card naming someone a Tutsi was a virtual death warrant.

Neighbors killed neighbors. People fled to churches, only to have frightened pastors turn them over to the killers.

Trapped in the middle of one of the worst humanitarian crises of the twentieth century, Claire lived in fear, but God miraculously kept His promise to protect her. At one point, she was in a group of Tutsis attacked by a Hutu mob with machetes. Everyone around her was hacked to death before her eyes, but for some inexplicable reason one of the attackers—a man Claire had never met and would never see again—stopped the others from killing her. Another time, Claire was in an area attacked by militia forces with grenades. She was wounded and scarred, but she again survived.

When the genocide finally ended, Claire was amazed to be alive. She knew that the voice she had heard in prison was that of the true God, and unlike the human males in her life, He had kept His promise to protect and care for her. Claire became a Christian and discovered the unconditional love she had been longing for all her life.

God immediately began to speak to Claire's heart. As she watched peace return to her country and the people begin to rebuild their lives, Claire felt God telling her to let go of her wounds. In order to heal, Claire needed to forgive her enemies: first her father, then the teacher, and then the men who came so close to killing her. Finally, God called her to do the hardest thing of all: forgive the boy who had left her pregnant and alone almost a decade before.

Claire struggled most with the idea of forgiving the father of her child. For years, she had held a grudge and dreamed of revenge—what she would say if she met him on the street, what she would do to him if she had the chance. But God continued to bring her messages about forgiveness, and Claire finally found peace. Her desire for revenge disappeared, and for the first time in her life she felt freed from her own emotions.

Not long after that, she saw her child's father on the street. Claire approached him, and instead of being angry and bitter, she told him she forgave him for abandoning her. She explained how God had protected her and her son (who had been safe in Burundi during the massacres). Claire's forgiveness touched her old boyfriend's heart, and because of her testimony, he too became a Christian.

After witnessing the power of forgiveness in her life and others, Claire dedicated her life to serving God. She began to work for Youth With a Mission (YWAM) in Rwanda, showing others the power of Christ's love and His ability to transform individuals. She discovered her calling in the words of Paul in 2 Corinthians 1:3–4: "Praise be to the God and Father of our Lord Jesus Christ, the Father of compassion and the God of all comfort, who comforts us in all our troubles, so that we can comfort those in any trouble with the comfort we ourselves have received from God."

Today, Claire works with people suffering from or living with AIDS, which is ravaging Africa. She considers it a delight to comfort and serve people, young and old, at the end of their lives. She thanks God that the cycle of anger and revenge has been broken in her life, and that the reconciliation she experienced is being used by God to help others.

All this is from God, who reconciled us to himself through Christ and gave us the ministry of reconciliation: that God was reconciling the world to himself in Christ, not counting men's sins against them. And he has committed to us the message of reconciliation.

(2 Corinthians 5:18–19)

joy churchill
SILENT NO MORE

Joy's father was a pastor. Her mother's father was a pastor. Her mother's only brother was a pastor. Her father's father was a pastor. Even Joy's father's *mother* was a pastor. In short, she grew up surrounded by courageous saints proclaiming the gospel.

Few words escaped Joy's lips, however. She was terribly shy and convinced that no one liked her. If the gospel was to go forth, it would have to go through someone else. Joy loved Jesus and wanted to serve Him, but she spent most of her days trying to remain unnoticed. On the best days, she was tongue-tied.

College and dorm life brought out the worst of Joy's insecurities. On the weekends, she hid from the crowd by studying in the lounge. Imagine her surprise when she was approached by a nice guy named Frank. One evening he plopped down next to her, leaned over, and kissed her. Joy was stunned but also pleased. She actually felt desirable and off her guard when she was with him.

The next day Frank invited Joy to his room to study, and she agreed. They did study . . . for a while. Then they touched, and Frank held her and kissed her. He gave Joy all she had been longing for: attention, affection, and acceptance. For just a moment it all seemed right. But the moment tilted and lurched. Frank moved much faster than Joy wanted. This was no time to remain silent. She pushed away from Frank, saying, "No."

When Frank ignored her protest, she thought, *Didn't I say it forcefully enough?* She tried to resist, make him stop, but he was much stronger, and her words were not enough. The world around her twisted and distorted. Within the space of a few minutes, Frank had taken everything.

After it was over, Joy found herself curled up alone at the back entrance of the dorm, shaking uncontrollably. A tornado of feelings ripped through her. *I should have yelled out,* she thought. *It's my fault.*

As the cold from the concrete steps seeped up through Joy's body, the Deceiver crept out to infiltrate and poison her mind. She had survived physical rape; now the devil intended to destroy the rest of her life. He whispered to her, "You're dirty and worthless. You're stained and rejected. You're weak and pathetic."

As the days passed, the lies drove deep into Joy's soul and began to grow out of control. She couldn't get things straight in her head. She began to hear all the accusations in first person: *I am dirty and worthless. . . . I am weak and pathetic.*

Angry and ashamed for not being pure enough, strong enough, verbal enough, Joy began making choices based on the lies she now believed to be true. She would never trust again. She would regain control. She found that if she acted a certain way, there were lots of boys interested in her, and one by one, she began to give herself to them. Each time, Joy found a moment of acceptance. When she said yes, she felt a few minutes of control. But Joy knew she'd left a piece of herself with each guy. Each time there seemed to be less of her to give. And the part that remained she hated with a passion.

It was a vicious circle. The more Joy lived the lies, the more she confirmed them, and the more she believed the lies, the more she lived them.

One Sunday Joy woke up in a strange apartment. She didn't know where she was or whom she'd been with—if anyone. Joy couldn't even find her belongings. The next night she begged God to take her life. She couldn't continue her current life but wasn't even strong enough to leave it. But God spoke to her heart and gently led her a different way.

The next morning, Joy withdrew from school, determined to leave the memory of the woman she had become far behind. She began attending church regularly and moved into a house with committed Christian girls. But no matter where she went, she found herself entrenched in the same thought patterns. The more Joy involved herself with godly men and women, the more self-hate grew in her. Her autopilot was stuck on defensive, making others her judge and jury. Her childhood of quiet shyness couldn't touch the alienation she knew.

Graciously, God nudged Joy toward a new home among a group of Christians who knew how to live honestly with their pasts and the present. On one hand she felt refreshed, but on the other she was resistant to the free and forgiven lives they were living. That didn't work with her plan. She wanted to punish herself rather than let Christ set her free. Her anger brewed.

But God still had His plan for Joy. He began to speak to her in many ways, but especially through the life of a friend—a

Rollerblading buddy named Connie. Each week, as the side-walks rolled under their feet, Connie talked about what was going on in her life. Connie spoke of a God with unfailing, unending love. A God of infinite compassion, but also a God of unbridled passion. His love and grace were neither forced nor reluctant; they flowed freely from His being into Connie . . . and Joy. This God took every lash of punishment; each drop of His blood He'd shed for all of Connie's sins . . . and Joy's.

This was the truth that would ultimately set Joy free. This truth said Joy was made pure and holy by His blood and that His perfect Spirit dwelled in her—something no man could ever take away, no matter what he did to her body. This truth said she could never add to or earn what He had done by pun-ishing herself. This truth said Joy was not rejected—she was accepted, fully adopted as a daughter of the King.

But His message didn't stop there. No longer did Joy have to believe she was disqualified from serving Him. She didn't have to be silent or stay on the shelf like a broken toy so she wouldn't be a disgrace or do further damage to the kingdom. Now she was free to do some damage *for* the Kingdom!

As Joy finally realized she was forgiven, a new passion began to burn in her life. A flame of desire grew hotter and hotter to share His message of grace, love, and forgiveness with others. Joy would remain tongue-tied no longer.

Often at night before Joy goes to sleep, she imagines the roars of praise as God's children worship before His throne. Yet in the midst of the celebration, God hears a silence. Looking over the crowd, He sees an empty space, room for just one more, one more life that needs to hear of His love.

For her, Joy will not stay silent.

For Zion's sake I will not keep silent,
    for Jerusalem's sake I will not remain quiet,
till her righteousness shines out like the dawn,
    her salvation like a blazing torch.

                                        (Isaiah 62:1)

WEEK SEVEN JOURNAL

—◆—

✦ What lies from Satan might be leading you into sinful and destructive choices?

✦ Do you feel in any way that your past has disqualified you to serve Jesus in the future?

✦ Does the Bible say that is true or a lie?

✦ How did you meet Jesus Christ?

✦ What Bible verse or passage of Scripture has been most meaningful to you this week? Why?

jaime

DESERT RAINBOW

{ ight years ago, God lit a fire for missions in Jaime's soul. How often does that happen to twelve-year-old kids? Jaime clearly remembers that day. She was sitting in the back of the church pretending not to hear the guest speaker's call to "go into all nations, preaching and teaching." But God didn't allow those words to pass by. Jaime's ears burned with the speaker's exhortation, and her heart desired to follow it.

It sounds simple, but Jaime just began to follow God's call. Every summer from then on, God opened the doors for her to go on short-term mission trips to Ecuador, Kenya, and many other countries. With each trip, Jaime's spirit warmed even more for the needs of people in other nations.

After high school, Jaime wanted a longer-term perspective on her missions work. She wanted to be sure her desire wasn't based on the thrill of high-energy, short-term, in-and-out experiences. So she boarded a plane to serve a missionary family in Lebanon as nanny for a year. She was going to see and learn from missionaries in the field and immerse herself gently in another culture while living with Americans.

Six months into her year, however, due to other circumstances, Jaime had moved to Jordan, was living on her own,
eating strange things (such as shish kebabs dipped in plain
yogurt), and trying her best to memorize and form foreign
sounds with her tongue. Jaime had enrolled in a two-year
Arabic program designed to prepare missionaries for the field.
She was gaining another perspective, all right.

Even though God graciously opened door after door for
Jaime on that journey, she walked through each of them literally shaking in her boots. After all, she was just eighteen years
old, fresh out of high school, and used to being snugly rooted
in her church and life. She had abandoned everything she
found comforting to follow God into a strange land. E-mail
and snail mail were still available to keep her connected to
home, but it wasn't the same as living there.

When Jaime had gone to Lebanon, the transition was difficult, but she had an amazing Christian family there who felt
familiar and comfortable. Jordan, however, was a completely
different experience. Jaime felt utterly alone. For the first year,
homesickness threw her into dark hours of depression. Her
journals reflect how God carried her through.

Journal Entry: 8.30.01

> God, I go to bed crying and wake up every morning the
> same. I desperately need you. You are my only hope. And
> because of your love, I know it will be okay. This past year
> has been filled with ups and downs and I don't even know
> what I am doing. Or why you've chosen me. Or if you even
> have. . . .

Drinking the sand of loneliness in the desert made Jaime thirst even more for the living water of her Lord and Savior. She knew she'd die without it. How parched she grew from her longing for home! Yet when she needed to know she wasn't alone, God always showed her He was there. So many times Jesus' living water washed over her.

For example, one day Jaime was struggling through her quiet time. Her mind kept wandering back to how deserted she felt. Her Bible reading that day happened to be about Noah and the Flood. When Jaime came to the part where God set a rainbow in the heavens as a sign of His everlasting covenant, all she could think was, *I haven't seen a rainbow in ages.* Living in the desert doesn't exactly lend itself to that phenomenon!

Jaime found herself desiring that rainbow all day. She realized how often she'd taken God's symbol of promise for granted in her home skies. Jaime's heart ached for home and for rain.

Later that same day she was in a car with a group of Muslim friends, and drops of rain began to slowly beat on the hood. As they drove on, the rain picked up. Just when the rain had almost stopped, there, stretching across the sky, was the most glorious rainbow she'd ever seen. It touched the ground on both sides. Everyone in the car was ecstatic and yelling; several of them had never seen one. But Jaime sat in silence and the tears began to flow. Overwhelmed, she knew God loved her so much that in the desert He had sent her a rainbow.

How often do God's people miss His messages of love and comfort? Though they find His voice in Scripture, nature also cries out not only His glory, but His amazing love. How tender yet magnificent is His love for His children. Yes, God wanted Jaime to give her all for Him; yes, He wanted her to lay down her life for Him. But when she was despondent, He comforted her. His presence and joy gave Jaime strength for the journey.

Journal Entry: 12.21.02

I can't believe that after two years of studying Arabic in Jordan that it's time for me to go home. I am going to board the plane today a completely different girl (or should I say woman) than I was.

Earlier this evening, I visited with more friends to say our good-byes. I don't even know how to put into words how much I have grown to love these people. I am going to miss them so much! Dear God, my heart is breaking. Even Mohammad broke down and cried when I got ready to leave. I handed him a special "book." I wrapped it so he couldn't see what it was. I pray that he reads it.

Though Jaime is no longer overseas, her heart to share the gospel with people from other nations has never waned. A year ago, Virginia Commonwealth University didn't have an international student ministry. But then God put Jaime in the right place at the right time to start one. Now there are ten in the group. On Ash Wednesday of 2004, no less than sixty international students went to see *The Passion of the Christ* movie with Jaime and the group!

Today Jaime prays, "Thank You, Lord, for preparing me for this work. I so understand their culture shock, homesickness, and frustration with the language barrier. It's clear to me now why You allowed me to experience You so dramatically in my loneliness while on foreign soil. Let me be Your desert rainbow to those who are a long way from home."

The heavens declare the glory of God;
  the skies proclaim the work of his hands.
Day after day they pour forth speech;
  night after night they display knowledge.
There is no speech or language
  where their voice is not heard.
Their voice goes out into all the earth,
  their words to the ends of the world.
In the heavens he has pitched a tent for the sun.

(Psalm 19:1–4)

linda

A SURPRISING LINGUIST

Linda gave her heart to Jesus when she was nearly five years old, and she's been following His heart ever since—wherever that takes her. She lived overseas from age two to six. "My brother spent his first four birthdays in four different countries," she says. She has vivid memories of other cultures:

~ Going on German *volksmarches,* in which she walked through pine forests using a walking stick.
~ Living in Liverpool, England, with its hazy rain.
~ Buying kilts in Scotland.
~ Playing in a bamboo playhouse a gardener built for her in Bangladesh.

Her most vivid memories come from Bangladesh, where her family skirted rice paddy borders to go to a local church. "I saw *dokans* (market stalls), people eating and spitting beetle-nut juice, and shacks of plastic and metal barely holding together," Linda says. As much as she loved Bangladesh, though, Linda hated learning its language—Bengali. In fact, she ran away from the class, saying it was just too difficult.

For the most part, though, Linda loved her young life, experiencing many diverse cultures around the globe. But she dreaded leaving each place. "The hard part is the ripping feeling in your heart when you're always saying good-bye," she says. "The sorrow is never knowing when or if you will see a playmate again."

When Linda's family returned to the United States, they still embraced many cultures. "We used to joke that our house was IHOP—International House of People. Our guest book is full of unique names and languages, and my mom's recipe box resembles the index of an international atlas."

In high school, Linda organized a Teens For Life group, recruiting volunteers and teaching students about infanticide, abortion, and euthanasia. When the group focused on sexual purity, Linda stood in front of the student body and expressed her commitment to remain abstinent until marriage. "The hardest audiences were the students at my own high school," she says. "I couldn't just stand in front, speak, and then go home. I had to go to school with them every day."

After high school, God spoke to Linda through her parents. One summer after college, a graphic design and writing firm in Manhattan offered her a job. Linda envisioned herself in the job, living in the big city and enjoying a three-month stint in sunny Manhattan. But her parents wanted her to spend one summer at home, since she'd been away two others on overseas trips. Linda turned to Proverbs, specifically chapters 4 and 5, which talk about the wisdom of parents. She chose to heed their advice, letting the Manhattan job go.

When Linda found a job at home, it was a clerical position, filing and stapling papers. Still, Linda says, "One year later, I could look back and see the faithfulness of God's hand. My grandmother went home to heaven the next May, so the summer at home was the last time I could have spent with her."

The following summer, Linda worked for Trans World Radio in their studios in Russia and the Ukraine—a job far better than the Manhattan position.

After graduating from Dallas Theological Seminary, Linda spent two weeks in the Middle East. "I prayed God would give me open eyes and ears to see and hear those who needed Jesus' love," she relates. "I never expected to be invited to spend the night in an ethnic village, very close to a tense political border. There were times when I wondered what might happen to me there, but Jesus was right beside me. He provided three distinct times when I could tell the villagers about my belief in Jesus."

Linda's next life adventure will be Bible translation in Asia. She will train nationals to translate the Bible into what she calls their "heart language—a language that someone has spoken since he was a child, the language he laughs, cries, and prays in." She believes native believers are best equipped to translate the Bible since they are experts in their own language and culture.

Linda will spend time learning a national language as well as other minority languages. Veteran translators will mentor her. Once she completes both phases of training, she'll venture out to a culture that is yet to have a Bible translated into words they can read and understand.

Linda spends her training days in Asia learning about the culture, something her parents taught her to do from an early age. She lives in a high-rise apartment with no oven and no elevator. Just crossing the busy street has its own cultural and safety issues. "I must envision a host of winged guardians each time I pass the four-lane highway to get to the next bus stop," she says. "To cross the road, you must inch your way out of traffic, waiting for a cluster of pedestrians to form. Once your pedestrian cluster is large enough, you all move out—forcing the traffic to slow down. *Voila!* You, the angels, and the other pedestrians have crossed the street! Riding a bike requires the same trust."

One day in the country, Linda was invited by a local family to have some tea. The father offered Linda and her friends seating on handmade bamboo stools. He boiled the water as a courtesy for the visitors—to kill the bacteria—and offered it to them in rice bowls. The man's wife roasted sunflower seeds for the guests. In a letter back to the States, Linda described what happened next. The father "brought out a book. We were amazed! That book was the [New Testament] in their minority language. It seems that we had stumbled upon relatives, who had been part of the BIG family for twenty years!"

From Germany to Bangladesh, from England to the Middle East, from the United States to Asia, Linda has seen God's kingdom expanded. And now she's in the midst of expanding it further by God's grace, in a region unfriendly to Christianity.

Linda smiles, remembering God's paradoxes. "The irony and beauty of God's ultimate purpose is clear when I think about how I ran away from my Bengali language class saying, 'It's too hard.' I didn't study Bengali after that. Now, God uses me as a full-time linguist."

Linda has learned that with God anyone can find a way.

Do nothing out of selfish ambition or vain conceit, but in humility consider others better than yourselves. Each of you should look not only to your own interests, but also to the interests of others.

(Philippians 2:3–4)

holly davis

RELUCTANT MISSIONARY

When she was in Bible school, Holly used to tell her friends she would "rather throw up a thousand times than be a missionary." She imagined that if she even considered overseas missions, God would send her to the jungles of Africa. "I was sure that I would have to invent a language and weave my own clothes out of grass, because I could never walk around naked!" she laughs today.

Holly had other plans for her life. She had known ever since she committed her life to Christ when she was thirteen that she wanted to work with teenagers and young adults. She believed that God's plan was for her to get married and live in suburban America, leading the senior-high girls' ministry in a large church.

At first, Holly's expectation seemed accurate. She began studying at Moody Bible Institute to train for her calling. In her sophomore year, she met a fellow student, and they felt an instant connection. Stephen graduated and moved across the country to work in Christian radio, but he often returned to visit Holly, and the couple began to talk about how soon she could finish her degree so that they could get married.

The summer before her junior year, Holly arranged to work as a nanny near where Stephen lived, so that they could spend more time together. But shortly before Holly arrived, Stephen went through a series of emotionally painful situations with his job that led him to question almost everything in his life. "He was a wreck," Holly says, looking back. "After many late nights of conversations, Stephen told me that I could find someone better, and he walked out the door."

Holly felt as if her life had flipped upside down, and that God had wiped away any possibility for her to become who He created her to be. She returned to school depressed and angry. She considered taking a semester off, but she was afraid that if she left, she would never go back.

Yet even in her pain, Holly believed God must have had a bigger plan for her life, that all of her suffering and all of her college work must be for some greater purpose.

She did try to make one change to her life in acknowledgement of the hurt she suffered. Every student was required to study a foreign language, and Holly had chosen German because it was Stephen's native language. Determined to put all thoughts of her former love behind her, she marched to the registrar's office to change her language to French. But she discovered that the only available French class took place early in the morning, and German was offered in the middle of the day. She decided to take the more practical route and stayed with German.

As Holly continued through the first difficult year after her broken relationship, a missionary came to Holly's youth ministry class to talk about the need for youth leaders on U.S. military bases around the world. Holly's heart began to race. Was this what God wanted her to do with her German? Was this a way to serve Him? Working with American kids in Germany didn't sound like the wilderness of Africa.

In January 1999, Holly boarded a plane bound for Stuttgart, Germany, where she served as a youth missions intern for four months. Although it was not a lifelong commitment, Holly calls it her "first leap of faith for God. I came back a changed woman, with a bigger worldview and a slight passion for missions."

Yet Holly clung to the idea that she was not called to overseas work. She settled into another internship, this time with a church in Minnesota. Her life seemed to be moving toward the suburban church position she had always dreamed about when a permanent position for a senior-high girls' youth director opened up in a nearby town.

Holly says, "I believe we all have two choices in our lives that we constantly make: to grow closer to God or to stay where we are with Him." That Christmas, as she pondered the new job opportunity, Holly faced a crossroad. She could take the easy route and accept the job in the United States. Or . . . When Holly was honest with herself, she knew something had changed. The church job didn't sound appealing anymore. Holly was dreaming about Europe. Although she tried to put aside her doubts and secret longings, God would not let it go.

Holly's choice became even more difficult when, out of the blue, Stephen called her. He said only that he wanted to get together and talk, but in her heart, Holly believed that if she saw her former love, things would pick up where they had ended so abruptly eighteen months before. Confused, with her emotions tearing her apart, Holly fled to the prayer room of her church for what she describes as "a little honest talk with God." As she poured out her questions and concerns, the right path became clear. She was being called to grow closer to God. And that would take faith, sacrifice, and a few radical changes in what she had planned for her future.

"I handed Stephen back over to God and [accepted] my singleness," Holly says. "I knew what I was walking away from, and I told God that if He wanted me to marry someday, He would have to take care of it for me. I needed to go overseas and serve Him. I chose intimacy with Him, no matter what that looked like." Peace and assurance washed over her almost immediately.

Holly never did see Stephen. This next season of life was about only Holly and God. Perhaps one day she would marry, but for now, she had embraced the title she never dreamed of owning: single missionary.

Once Holly said yes to God's call, plans fell into place quickly. She continued to hear God whisper, "Pursue Europe," so in June of 2000, Holly joined Greater Europe Mission—an organization committed to assisting the peoples of Europe in building up the body of Christ. Before long, she found herself in Linz, Austria, helping the local church launch a youth ministry for Austrian teens.

It hasn't been easy to become fluent in a second language or to fit into a culture so different from what she knew. Yet looking back, Holly reflects, "I am here because God called me. My mind wanders back to the days when I claimed that I would never move overseas, and I have to smile. I am silenced when I think about how God so graciously picked me up, altered my path, and lovingly inscribed His desires onto my heart. God continues to radically change my heart and mold me into His woman."

Holly clings to a verse she discovered four years ago, when she was wounded by her broken relationship and uncertain of her future calling: "Does the LORD delight in burnt offerings and sacrifices / as much as in obeying the voice of the LORD? / To obey is better than sacrifice" (1 Sam. 15:22). Holly's obedience to God's call in her life has certainly caused her to sacrifice, but in the end, she knows her joy is far richer than anything she may have lost. She is a reluctant missionary no more.

Rejoice in the Lord always. I will say it again: Rejoice! Let your gentleness be evident to all.

(Philippians 4:4–5)

anne savage
HEART FOR THE WORLD

Nineteen-year-old Anne Savage met Jesus when she was young but truly internalized and personalized her relationship with Him more recently, as a teenager. That's when she started going on missions trips. She's been on one every summer since sixth grade. In North America, she's been to Missouri, Minnesota, and Mexico. In 2001, she went on her first overseas mission trip to Caracas, Venezuela. Focus on the Family's teen girl magazine *Brio* conducts an annual overseas trip and on a whim, Anne applied.

The trip was life-transforming: "For the first time in my life I was exposed to a new culture that needed God just as much as I did."

Anne remembers meeting an older woman after performing an evangelistic street play. "After the play, I felt drawn to her. She was adamant that she didn't need a personal relationship with Jesus Christ. She was fine with her Sunday-to-Sunday ritual of going to mass. I felt frustrated and defeated that I could not share God's love with her. Then it hit me that I needed to *show* God's love to her."

Through the interpreter, Anne asked the woman if she could give her a hug. She nodded. Anne wrapped her arms around the woman, who began to cry. "It was awesome to see that such a simple action was all she needed, and all it cost me was to cross the ocean and give her a hug!"

Another summer, Anne went to China—this time with Family Life Ministry's Hope for Orphans trip, where she helped with annual physicals for a large orphanage. She remembers her nerves as the plane began its descent. She was well aware of the laws preventing her from sharing her faith. But God comforted her. A small video screen in the cabin showed the passengers the illuminated runway. "All of a sudden, this huge, bright cross came into view on the screen. I kept looking, amazed that this would be so bright and tall for all to see. As we came closer, I realized that it was the runway lights, but it was a reminder to me that God was in control." She says seeing the illuminated runway cross was like hearing God say, "Anne, you are in My hands. I will protect you."

"From then on, I was so excited, I wasn't worried at all," she says. "We had several opportunities to share our faith. God truly worked in all our lives as well as in those who interacted with us." She especially remembers the orphans. "It was incredible to see all these little children looking at us with smiling faces. The language barrier didn't matter."

Being in a country where Christianity is discouraged and illegal, Anne sensed the Lord in a new way. "This was the first time I felt as if my faith was a huge factor in my life."

She's also seen God's protection and guidance in Normal, Illinois, where she lives with her family. The Savage family planted a church in 2000. "In three and a half years, we are busting at the seams of our building," she says. "It is so awesome to see such passionate people coming together and worshiping God."

For the past two years, Anne has been the church's vacation Bible school director, a job she started when she was seventeen. Even then, her desire was to see God touch not only the children, but also the leaders. "As we prayed prior to the event each night, everyone was focused on the kids. But at the end of the night, our prayer time was focused on each other. There were men and women crying, and God mended their broken hearts. I was blown away that God would use this event for little kids to touch the lives of the adults."

Just as God used a children's venue to touch children and adults alike, He used the face of a young Russian boy to change Anne's family forever. One day, someone handed Anne's mom a picture of Kolya, asking if she knew someone who could adopt him. Kolya's best friend, who came from the same orphanage, had been adopted by a family one mile from the Savages' home. When Kolya's friend could speak English, the first thing she said to her adopted family was "You need to find a home for my friend."

After much prayer and discussion, the Savage family decided to adopt Kolya, who shares an uncanny resemblance to the boys in their family. The whole family helped in the fundraising efforts to adopt the boy. Anne pioneered "Cooking for Kolya"; she cooked freezer meals and desserts and sold them to friends, family members, even teachers. She raised over a thousand dollars.

The journey to adopt Kolya was a faith-stretching time. Yet God provided through grants, gifts from strangers, and donations. "It became our motto that God owned cattle on a thousand hills. He only needed to sell a few cows to make this happen! We definitely saw the blessings of those cows."

Now, Anne is the eldest of five and is attending Taylor University. She has a yearning to take Jesus to Europe, particularly France. She loves singing worship songs to Jesus, experiencing His tangible presence.

The future? "My heart is to be involved in mission work. There is so much pain and emptiness out there. I have come to realize, though, that whatever plans I have, God is going to radicalize them! I cannot even fathom the amazing plans God has for me."

Therefore, I urge you, brothers, in view of God's mercy, to offer your bodies as living sacrifices, holy and pleasing to God—this is your spiritual act of worship. Do not conform any longer to the pattern of this world, but be transformed by the renewing of your mind.

(Romans 12:1–2)

niki mcdonnall
NO REGRETS

When Niki attended fifth-grade camp, she declared she wanted to be a missionary when she grew up. Her future husband, David McDonnall, made the same decision his fifth-grade year.

At Texas A&M, Niki served on a ministry team at Central Baptist Church that coordinated outreach to more than five hundred students. She led freshman Bible studies. Although a student, she was fully committed to working in her church and reaching out to nonbelievers. Still, she was burdened by her fifth-grade dream of becoming a missionary.

She fulfilled that dream by becoming a Journeyman missionary with the IMB (International Mission Board), a Southern Baptist missionary agency whose Journeyman program encourages young men and women to become missionaries. It sent her to the Middle East. She met David, also a Journeyman missionary, on a crowded Bethlehem Square in Israel amid the cacophony and mayhem of New Year's Eve celebrations.

Initially, neither wanted to serve in the Middle East, but

independently they fell in love with the Middle Eastern people and each other. Both became fluent in Arabic.

Stateside, two years later, David gave Niki a cookie cake with a frosted "I love you. Will you marry me?" written in Arabic. She said yes.

The couple enrolled in Southwestern Seminary in Fort Worth, Texas. While there, they were asked to lead a group of seminary students on a humanitarian aid trip for three weeks one summer to northern Iraq. Along with their dozen-member team, they celebrated their first wedding anniversary on Iraqi soil. Then they returned to Texas.

Because of the couple's fluency in the language and their hearts for Arab people, they were asked to suspend seminary and go to postwar Iraq full-time. Niki weighed her fears and consulted her pastor. In the end, she decided to place her trust in God despite Iraq's security issues. Showing the Iraqi people God's tangible love trumped her own fears for safety.

Amid the fury of almost daily terrorist acts against Americans, Niki and David relocated to Iraq to coordinate humanitarian aid for the Iraqi people. Letters home never indicated that she feared danger. Instead, Niki highlighted the work they were doing: interacting with the Iraqi people, delivering food and supplies, rebuilding war-torn schools, and locating water.

One afternoon, Niki, her husband, and three other missionaries spent time with several Iraqis who were subsisting in abject poverty. "We had a great day with them. They had been so welcoming. They were so eager for our help," Niki says. They concluded their time there by deciding to secure a site for a water purification plant for the desperate people they met.

On their way back, a car pulled alongside their vehicle. Within moments the car was sprayed with bullets from automatic weaponry and rocket-powered grenades. After the assailants fled the ambush, David called his supervisor in Jordan on a satellite phone. "We've all been shot," he said.

The five were transported to a nearby U.S. battlefield hospital. Niki remembers seeing David across the room; his injuries seemed minor. They spoke to each other.

"I love you," he said.

"I love you too," she mouthed.

"We're going to make it through this," he said. They were the last words she heard David speak before she succumbed to a drug-induced coma. Later, David died aboard an army helicopter. Four U.S. Army surgeons spent six hours trying to keep him alive. But Niki didn't know.

She woke up eight days later in a Texas hospital. Still hazy, the first person she asked for was David. Her family evaded her questions until finally she asked if he was mad at her. Then her family circled her hospital bed. Her father told her David had died the day after the car attack.

Now the lone survivor of the March 15, 2004, ambush, Niki faces life as an injured widow. She's recovering from over twenty gunshot and shrapnel wounds. Her list of bullet wounds is long. A bullet splintered her lower left leg, carving a hole so large the doctors thought they'd have to amputate. Amazingly, the leg was saved and the prognosis is that she will walk just months after the attack. She's hobbled from crutches to cane and will someday walk without assistance.

She lost three fingers on her left hand, leaving her with a middle finger and a thumb. It's been a difficult adjustment to make. "It's weird, but I keep forgetting those fingers aren't there. For twenty-six years I had them. So I reach to hold something, and it falls out of my hand. And I remember."

She also notes, "I've got several graze wounds on the back of my head. Another quarter inch and it would have been my life."

According to surgeons, one bullet entered her nose but then defied the laws of physics by exiting without hitting sinuses or brain tissue, her nose still intact. No reconstructive surgery, miraculously, is needed.

Despite the extensive injuries, Niki lives with hope and a desire to serve the Lord wherever He takes her. Her heart for the Iraqi people is evident, and she longs to see others willing to spend themselves for the sake of Jesus and His love for the Middle East. "We need to keep going to these places—to hard places, to sometimes violent places," she said. "They need help."

In the midst of a strong desire to see others go, Niki grieves the loss of her three friends and her husband. "In my human-ness, I definitely wish my husband had survived. I wish my friends had survived," she said. "But do I regret doing what we were supposed to do? I don't regret that at all. It was very clear that this is what we were meant to do."

Niki worries that people will lose courage because of her ordeal, forsaking overseas missionary service in war-ravaged countries. She longs for others to see past the violence to needy people. She wishes the evening news showed the humanity of people in other countries, not just the violent acts of a few.

She's often asked if she will go back to Iraq. "Eventually," she said. "Maybe." Niki admits, "It has been a hard road. There are still days I pray, 'Why?' I miss my husband."

Yet she has sensed God's presence even in her grief. "God has been so faithful. His mercies are new each morning. And that sense of His nearness has never left."

Still recovering, Niki wants to serve Christ wherever He leads her. "I'm not going tomorrow. But if God said, 'I want you to go back,' I'm not going to tell Him no." She points to her scarred body. "Not because of this."

———————————————————————————

I am convinced that neither death nor life, neither angels nor demons, neither the present, nor the future, nor any powers, neither height nor depth, nor anything else in all creation, will be able to separate us from the love that is in Christ Jesus our Lord.

(Romans 8:38–39)

———————————————————————————

WEEK EIGHT JOURNAL

＊— Besides Jesus, whom do you depend on most to fill your loneliness?

＊— What would your life look like if you could depend on Jesus for your "living water"?

＊— How do you see God using you in the lives of others?

＊— What people has God placed in your life? Are any of them lonely or outcasts or from foreign countries and need your ministry?

＊— What Bible verse or passage of Scripture has been most meaningful to you this week? Why?

yelena pytkina
GOD CAN MEET MY NEEDS

Yelena agreed to go to the new church only because she wanted to learn English. Born in the Russian city of Ulan-Ude in eastern Siberia, eighteen-year-old Yelena dreamed of attending a Russian university, where students must all pass a written and oral English exam. Quite a few Americans were in the church, Yelena knew, and she thought she could practice her English with them.

"I never thought that I [would] start going to that church and become a Christian," Yelena remembers. "But God knew how to draw me to Him."

This small, missionary-staffed church was nothing like the traditional Russian Orthodox Churches Yelena had attended in the past. A budding musician, Yelena was most affected by the music. She had never heard praise and worship music and was both shocked and excited when the English-speaking church used a guitar and backup instruments to praise God.

Yelena became friends with the American missionaries, who not only shared their music and taught her English but also introduced her to new ideas about God. Yelena learned how God loved her so much that he sent His own Son as a personal sacrifice just for her. She discovered she could have a personal relationship with God, and that He wanted to have a personal relationship with her. Yelena had never felt the presence of God as clearly as she did in that church.

When her new friends invited her to a home group to learn more about the Bible, Yelena accepted eagerly. That night, she says, "The Holy Spirit touched me in such a way that I felt Him. I felt as if I was held by someone, but there was no one hugging or even touching me. I was wrapped in God's love and warmth."

At first, Yelena's parents were opposed to their daughter's new passion for Jesus Christ. They were concerned that the foreign church Yelena had joined was a cult, and they prevented her from attending more home groups. Although she struggled with their decision, Yelena obeyed her parents' wishes. She continued to grow as a Christian by attending the Sunday services, and burdened by the knowledge that her parents did not share her faith in Christ, Yelena prayed every night that her mother would become a Christian.

Although she knew that she should pray for her father's salvation as well, Yelena couldn't at first. Like many men in that region, Yelena's father suffered from alcoholism. He had been cold, distant, and sometimes violent throughout Yelena's childhood. "I was scared of my dad," she says. "I couldn't talk to him. I couldn't trust him. There were sad moments in my life when I would cry, and there was no one in my family to support me."

But as Yelena continued to grow as a Christian, God continued to move her toward forgiveness. Reading her Bible one day, Yelena came to Matthew 5:44, where Jesus instructed His

followers to "love your enemies and pray for those who perse-
cute you."

Who are my enemies? Yelena asked herself. She knew the
answer: Jesus was telling her to forgive her father.

It took time and a lot of prayer, but eventually Yelena was
able to let go of the pain of her childhood, and she began praying for her father. Two years later, Yelena's father and mother
began attending her church.

With her family's blessing, Yelena answered God's call to
full-time ministry. When she was twenty-four, she packed her
belongings and made the four-day train journey from Siberia
to Moscow, Russia's capital city, to join the Youth With A
Mission team. Today, she leads worship, serves as a translator
and secretary, and disciples new Christians from around the
world.

Being a Russian missionary is not easy. Yelena does not
receive a salary for the work she does with YWAM; like most
others, she relies on private support. But the Russian economy
is struggling, and many people have a hard time feeding their
families, much less supporting missionaries. With most of the
Christians in Russia being new believers (the former commu-
nist regime did not allow Christian churches to evangelize for
many years), Russian families do not have a history or real
understanding of tithing or giving. They assume that someone else—the government or foreign supporters—will pay to
build back the Russian church that was neglected for so long.

But this is often not the case. Many pastors work full-time
jobs in addition to their ministries, and most Russian missionaries do not receive support from overseas sponsors. Yelena
knows that she could make a salary elsewhere, but she also
knows that she is where God wants her to be. She is content to

depend entirely on God to meet her needs. "God never lets me down in terms of provision of food and clothes. He is always faithful in these little things," she says with confidence.

God has been faithful not only to meet Yelena's financial needs, but He also protects her physically. The city of Moscow can be dangerous. Because of the economic instability and a growing drug problem, violent crime is common; Moscow streets are not considered safe after dark. Yet Yelena and her fellow missionaries often must walk home late at night after evening church services or meetings.

One night, as Yelena walked home with five other women, a group of six drunk Russian men armed with knives stopped the group and demanded money. Three of the girls ran, and Yelena started to follow them. But the Holy Spirit stopped her, and she realized that two of her friends—international missionaries who did not speak Russian—were still trapped by the men. Knowing that the girls were in much more danger if they did not understand their assailants, Yelena returned to the situation and acted as a translator. After giving up their money, the girls eventually fled together. The men chased them all the way to the place where they were living, but all six missionaries escaped unharmed.

Yelena is now entering her fourth year as a pioneer missionary in a country rediscovering Christianity, and she continues to seek the Lord's guidance for what He wants her to do. Her family situation is still not perfect—Yelena's father has not yet made a profession of faith in Christ, and he still drinks and is sometimes violent—but Yelena sees the difference her prayers have made.

Her work with YWAM continues to blossom, and Yelena has seen many new Christians in Russia grow in their faith because of her efforts. Her parents are the primary financial supporters of her ministry, and Yelena's mother is now a passionate Christian and a strong prayer warrior. With their help and the support of a growing Russian Christian population, Yelena will continue to be obedient to her call to spread the gospel all over the world, while letting God meet her every need.

Christ died for sins once for all, the righteous for the unrighteous, to bring you to God.

(1 Peter 3:18)

---

virginia

HEARING THE VOICE OF GOD

For Virginia, the hardest moments came when she believed she couldn't hear the voice of God.

During her first overseas missions trip—two weeks in Brazil with a church group her parents led—fourteen-year-old Virginia discovered a passion for ministry. "It was the first time I saw broken people weep in their need for Christ or [with their] arms lifted in worship," she remembers. "I saw the poor and made friends who speak a language I do not know. Nothing could have prepared me for the lives I saw there, and something changed inside me, flaming my desire to do the ministry of Jesus."

But Virginia faced a special challenge in serving God on the mission field. She was born deaf and has lived her entire life in silence. Her speech is often unintelligible to those who do not know her. Therefore, from the moment she felt the call to missions, she doubted it. How could God use her to preach His message of salvation?

Satan attacked Virginia with her physical weaknesses, filling her with feelings of loneliness and helplessness. "I felt as if I was rejected by life," Virginia explains. "I was in tears, battling strong lies and thoughts tormenting me from the evil one. I believed that I needed ears to hear the voice of God."

Virginia spent two long, difficult years struggling with her disability, feeling worthless. She resented the hardships of being deaf; like most girls, she wanted to fit in with her friends and classmates. Even more, she wanted to be a missionary, and she couldn't see how that was possible.

Finally, one night as she lay in bed feeling torn apart and broken, she saw a vision of the Lord. She fell to her knees as Jesus stood before her, and an amazing thing happened: she heard Him speak. "Virginia," He said, "I am willing to be yours."

Her depression lifted instantly. She could hear Jesus! She might not be able to use her physical ears to hear the sounds of the world around her, but her spirit could still hear. God spoke directly to Virginia's heart, intimately connecting her to Himself.

A few months after her encounter with God, Virginia left for her second summer missions trip, this time to Mexico with her youth group. Again her heart was drawn to the people she met, those who suffered so much and were so eager to experience the love of Christ. On that trip Virginia began to understand God's calling for her life. In an evening church service, the pastor announced that instead of preaching, he wanted to give each member of the congregation time to spend alone with God. Virginia went outside and sat in the soft summer grass. She waited, and in time she felt God again speaking to her spirit. "Virginia, you are My chosen servant. I call you. I will go before you. Come with Me to the corners of the earth."

It was unmistakable. God wanted her, Virginia, to be a missionary, to travel the globe for the rest of her life to share the good news and saving message of Jesus Christ.

Yet again, Virginia wrestled with her calling. She doubted her abilities and asked herself over and over, *Am I willing to go into a world where I cannot hear the languages? To be a light in the darkness, a sheep among wolves? Do I believe that the Holy Spirit will overcome my deafness, my speech . . . to let me preach?*

She found her answer in the Bible. In Matthew 10:19–20, Jesus told His disciples, "Do not worry about what to say or how to say it. At that time you will be given what to say, for it will not be you speaking, but the Spirit of your Father speaking through you."

Comforted by Jesus' promise, Virginia accepted God's call. After high school, she enrolled in Adventure In Missions' First Year Missionary Program. She moved to the bleak inner city of Philadelphia, Pennsylvania, where she ministered to her neighbors in a crime-filled, drug-infested area. Although she could not listen for signs of the often-present danger, Virginia spent hours on street corners. Although the people she served could not understand what she said, Virginia connected powerfully with everyone she met. Heroin addicts and homeless people found unconditional love in Virginia's eyes and hands. They found comfort as Virginia prayed for them.

From Philadelphia, Virginia continued to travel the globe to spread the good news of Jesus Christ. After short-term projects in Panama and West Virginia, she felt God call her to a new mission. When she was only twenty-two, Virginia began to lead groups of Christian high school students to England, Ireland, and the Dominican Republic. The teenagers in her charge did not understand sign language, yet God worked in their relationships, and while sometimes Virginia struggled to understand what was being said, she mentored, taught, and cared for the girls in ways that changed their lives and hers.

Wherever she went, Virginia's passion for Christ touched not only the people she served, but also her fellow missionaries. One friend explains, "Her presence has never ceased to change lives. As others see her stepping out in faith and living her faith regardless of her deafness, they are encouraged and challenged to step out as well."

During her year of service in Philadelphia, Virginia had met a fellow missionary with a passion for the poor and the unreached. They fell in love and were married shortly after.

God began to show the couple new ways to reach out to people who did not know the gospel. During a two-week trip to China, Virginia and her new husband met students who had to study the Bible in secret because the government prohibits practicing Christianity. Virginia's heart, always so in tune with God, felt His call to China to minister to the persecuted church there. Once again, she took a leap of faith and followed. After months of prayer, Virginia and her husband left for China.

Today, they are missionaries in a country that does not allow missionaries, sharing the gospel despite the physical risks.

Virginia continues to see her deafness as something that God uses to change lives, including hers, rather than something that separates her from God or the people around her. She clings to the words of the apostle Paul in Acts 20:24: "I consider my life worth nothing to me, if only I may finish the race and complete the task the Lord Jesus has given me—the task of testifying to the gospel of God's grace."

Virginia can hear the one voice that matters, and she is following it.

Preach the Word; be prepared in season and out of season; correct, rebuke and encourage—with great patience and careful instruction.

(2 Timothy 4:2)

---

li paʃanɡ
EVEN IF NOT

The living Buddha—who lived a mountain journey away—gave Li Pasang her name when she was an infant. She grew up under the shadow of his mountains in a community known for its hopelessness. So when, as a young woman, Pasang found a hard lump near her breast—the breast that nursed her firstborn son—she resigned herself to death.

Still, she approached a foreign doctor for his advice. The smile on her thin, pale face showed she dared to hope that the lump she found was nothing. When she entered the clinic, her one-year-old baby clung to her back in a makeshift sling. She delivered the baby to her mother and took her place in line—a line so long it wound around the mayor's office.

When she finally saw the doctor, she said matter-of-factly, "I have something the matter with my chest."

The doctor reached for some medicine, but she stopped him. "No, it's not pain, it's a lump—just under my skin. Here."

A translator relayed the doctor's words: "She has a mass—hard and immovable." The doctor poked and prodded to make a more complete examination. The hopelessness that infused

Pasang's village fixed its hold around her neck like a tightening noose. Yet the nice doctor assured her that hope was not lost. If she could get the mass removed at the hospital, things might turn out well. He encouraged her to come with him to the city, where she could be treated and possibly cured.

While Pasang's husband and small son waited in her village, she began the long and difficult journey. It was not easy. For Pasang's entire life, her sole means of transportation had been her feet. She'd never been in an automobile before, and its motion made her violently ill. Gripping her stomach, she fought to keep her food down, eventually losing the battle. The winding, tortuous roads mocked her. She felt her lump as vomit stung her tonsils. No hope.

Through perilous roads and towns decimated by the SARS epidemic, Pasang held her stomach. She didn't pray. She didn't know she could. The doctor with the pale, worried face gave her some medicine. He said it would help her stomach, but it didn't. On and on they drove, up hills, through villages foreign to her. Li Pasang had never before ventured beyond her village, beyond the eyes of the living Buddha.

A student traveling with them became ill from the Yak butter tea they'd had for breakfast. After seeing both women's pained faces, the doctor pulled over to let them rest. When they began their nauseating journey again, a police car flanked them. The officer shouted, "You must be out of this region at this moment! We are closing the road." SARS had reached yet another territory.

The three travelers stopped in a high mountain village near a clear lake. They approached the village's center. It was eerily calm. Only one lone lady walked the vacant street. "You'd better leave now, or you will be stuck here," she said.

"No one can leave after tomorrow." Another town closed by SARS.

Pasang watched the mountains, her stomach eventually settling after a second round of medicine. In another village nearly closed by SARS, they stayed in the house of a kind stranger, woke up early, and continued their journey, hoping to reach the hospital before the roads closed. Along the journey the only people they saw were nurses and doctors in scrubs and face masks. Had they left one day later, they'd have been trapped many miles away from the hospital.

The trio arrived in the city at nightfall. When the doctor showed Pasang to her hospital room, he explained that she needn't be afraid of the leprous-looking patients. "They have the scars of leprosy, but they are healed. Do not be afraid."

She was afraid—not of the scarred people but of the battery of tests she had to endure. Her first full day in the hospital, her first encounter with such a building, confirmed cancer. Pasang sobbed as she absorbed the weight of the word. The doctor scheduled an operation and arranged for her sister to keep her company in the long days ahead; family members provided the only nursing care.

Before her surgery, the doctor shared Jesus with Pasang. He told her about His life, His death, and His resurrection. He said that Jesus loved Pasang.

"What you are saying sounds like the words of the living Buddha," she responded. Yet the living Buddha gripped her village in fear, warning that if a villager inadvertently killed a bug while plowing he might end up a lesser being.

The doctor continued to share Jesus with Pasang as well as discuss her condition. "People in the countryside believe cancer is incurable, don't they?"

She nodded.

"It's not incurable. There are still things we can do. The treatments are difficult, but you are young and strong, and you have a baby boy. You should try. Don't give up. I will help you all I can."

A few days later, the doctor told Pasang about a God who came to help the helpless. She stared at the wall, the words lacking impact. The doctor continued, sharing how Jesus suffered. Eventually, a smile crept to Pasang's dry lips. "Doctor," she said, "may we believe in Jesus? Are we allowed?"

"Of course you may. But will you? Do you love Him? Do you believe?"

Pasang did not reply. She smiled again and looked at her sister.

The next day her lump was removed, and she commenced chemotherapy. The doctor then had to leave Pasang because of his commitments back home. During the chemotherapy sessions, though, the doctor's words about Jesus made their way to Pasang's heart. Like a bud slowly blooming, she believed. And then her sister believed. Elusive hope came to them both through the gentle hands of Jesus.

During a brief chemotherapy respite, they returned to her village—a place untouched by Christianity—and shared Jesus with the villagers. Thirty families gave their hearts to Him, angering local officials, who deemed their gatherings cultic. The new Christians, including Pasang's husband, were blamed for the village's misfortunes. Former friends ridiculed Pasang publicly for daring to betray the living Buddha. The community that once embraced Pasang now shunned her. When the Chinese New Year came, Pasang and the other Christian families refused to participate in ritual sacrifices, furthering their isolation and persecution.

Still, today Pasang smiles. A new Christian, she thanks God for the cancer as she endures chemotherapy. "I am glad Jesus loved me enough to allow the tumor so that I could hear about Him through a doctor."

Thirty families who lived under the shadow of the living Buddha's mountain are thankful too.

But you are a chosen people, a royal priesthood, a holy nation, a people belonging to God, that you may declare the praises of him who called you out of darkness into his wonderful light.

(1 Peter 2:9)

ςara

LEARNING TO SURRENDER

Spring break of her freshman year, Sara sat alone in her dorm room. Life had become unbearable, and she pleaded with God to let her die. As she prayed for God to take her, a song came over the radio. Between sobs Sara heard, "He climbed the highest hill to save you." The words pierced the young woman, and she begged God for something she'd never before asked: "Teach me how to surrender my life to You."

Surrender came hard. After years of rebelling, Sara doubted that God was even willing to provide for her, whether it was relationally, spiritually, financially, or emotionally. But she has since learned her heavenly Father delights in His children and He answers prayer—even if it's shrouded in skepticism.

The summer following Sara's freshman year in college should have been her best ever. A cruise line in Alaska hired her as a stewardess. She found a house with fifteen other young seasonal workers, met a great Christian guy—David—started dating, got pregnant, and then got dumped.

Sara was devastated. She was hundreds of miles from home, and David didn't want anything to do with her. Sara quickly realized that God had allowed her to be stripped of everything—except His provision.

Out of a house of fifteen, He gave Sara eight believing friends to cover her in prayer, grace, and love. Not only did God lavish her with companionship, He gave her a best friend named Joy. She loved Sara through late-night panic attacks, anger, grief, and continued doubt. Joy placed her trust and life in the hands of the Father, and Sara slowly learned to do the same.

When summer ended, Sara headed back to Seattle. By God's grace she didn't have to go home alone. Five of her summer roommates also happened to live in Seattle. They continued to meet with Sara to study the Bible and pray for her. They stood by her while she wrestled with the most difficult decision of her life: whether to keep her baby or give it up for adoption.

A mom was the only thing Sara had ever wanted to be. But secretly, she thought God wanted to punish her. And what would be more painful than making her give up her first child? Even though Sara believed God would make her pay for all her poor choices, she still decided to trust Him. After all, she hadn't done so well without Him! Sara wanted to do His will, no matter what.

She began preparing herself for "His" answer by reading up on adoption. The first book she read was about a young Christian girl who was raped and became pregnant. It seemed only logical, Sara thought, that she would give up the baby. Yet she didn't, even though the baby was conceived in shame. For the first time Sara realized that God had already paid her penalty. He didn't want or need to punish her. All He wanted was to show her His mercy and grace.

Yet even with all the grace and mercy in the world, Sara wasn't sure she could afford a child. She started attending meetings at the adoption agency. At one of the meetings, a young girl spoke about giving up her own baby. She struggled with the same question, "Can I provide for a child?" She finally concluded, "I wasn't going to be able to buy my kid Nike shoes. And I wanted my baby to have parents who could."

As Sara listened to her story, Matthew 6 popped in her head: "Do not worry about your life, what you will . . . wear. Will [God] not . . . clothe you?" (vv. 25, 30). Sara walked out of the meeting not willing to give her baby up for adoption because of shoes. That day, Sara decided to keep her daughter; Grace would be her name.

At last she was able to settle happily into her pregnancy. As her third trimester commenced, Sara began looking forward to the day Grace would be born. Then, three days before she was scheduled to give birth, David called. He said, "Isn't it ironic that if you were the kind of person who would give up a baby, then you would be a person I could be with." Although he was obviously attempting to use and manipulate her again, Sara was consumed by fears of being alone without a man and raising a baby without a father. All she could muster was, "I'll think about it."

Confused, Sara longed for a quiet place where she could sort things out with her heavenly Father. She drove around for hours. Finally, she found the place she was looking for: a bench by the ocean. Exhausted, Sara sat at the water's edge, sobbing and asking God for guidance.

As she cried, she thought of Abraham leading Isaac to the altar. He was willing to give his son away because it was God's will. Sara cried out, "Is this what You are asking of me? If I give my baby away, how will You bring her back to me?" Afraid and unsure, Sara returned home. Then she called David and agreed to give the baby away. The next morning he picked her up to sign the papers.

A stack of legal work was waiting for her when she arrived. The first page read: "I agree I am unable to offer relational, financial, psychological, and emotional stability for a child at this time. Therefore, it is in the best interest of my child to be given to a family who can. . . ." At the bottom of the page was a line for Sara's signature.

She picked up the pen, but even if she could give away the baby emotionally, she couldn't do it physically. Sara literally couldn't put the pen to paper. She left without signing anything. Later, as she sat at home rubbing her belly, she wondered if God had sent an angel to restrain her hand.

Two days later, Grace was born. All five of Sara's girl-friends from her summer in Alaska were there. For nine months they had held up their lanterns of learned surrender and guided her toward a trustworthy God. That day Sara knew fully that God's provision surrounded her.

Sara periodically still finds herself doubting God's care for her, but her distrust is shrinking. Righteous women continue to embrace the young mother with prayer, encouragement, and guidance. It is because of God's merciful gifts, she says, that she has learned to trust Him. She is able to say confidently God is not only her Savior, He is the Lord of her life.

Today, Sara has been married four years to a devoted Christ-follower. Jason loves to say that it was her compassionate heart that drew him to her. She insists he fell in love with a little brown-haired girl named Grace. Three years ago, Jason adopted Grace and is now raising her as his own.

When we think about sisters sold out for Jesus, we often think only of women who leave their homelands and go far away to minister. But Sara, pressing hard after the heart of God, discovered what it meant to surrender and rely solely on her Lord while answering one of God's highest callings: motherhood.

Consider it pure joy, my brothers, whenever you face trials of many kinds, because you know that the testing of your faith develops perseverance. Perseverance must finish its work so that you may be mature and complete, not lacking anything.

(James 1:2–4)

---

irene gut
THE RESCUER

Irene Gut began her teenage years during a very dark time in history: Hitler had just become chancellor and president of Germany. Like every teenage girl, Irene had dreams. She thought maybe she would like to be an actress, though she felt plain and unattractive.

She could be found climbing trees and riding horses. Boys weren't of interest, as she found herself daydreaming of partaking in heroic acts, saving lives, and sacrificing herself to save others. With such lofty ambitions, romance took a back seat and sounded rather dull. Adventure was set deeply in her heart.

But Irene also knew that there wasn't much in the way of adventure for a young girl in the 1930s. She saw, however, that there were ways she could serve locally. Her mother and father were always showing mercy toward their out-of-luck neighbors, wounded animals, and even the Gypsies, the town outcasts. Irene knew she could help her sisters prepare baskets of food for the poor and sick. And she could do more; with her parents' blessing, Irene decided to join the Red Cross as a volunteer candy striper.

She learned first aid and how to tend to medical emergencies. During her time at the hospital, Irene grew to admire the nuns in their service to God; she thought she would like to do that. Her father was surprised and advised her to first go to nursing school at St. Mary's Hospital in Radom. If she still felt called after that, her father said she could study to be a nun.

Irene began nursing school in 1938, when she was just sixteen. She was lonely and afraid to be in a strange city with no family nearby. Irene immersed herself in her books.

Soon rumors of war began. Hitler wanted to reclaim Poland. Irene's parents wanted her to come home if war was indeed imminent. But Irene didn't listen. Living in Poland, she knew some of her country's suffering and was taught to be proud of her heritage. Though the dark regime of Hitler was on the rise, Irene knew little of politics and what was about to take place. She informed her parents, "If Hitler tries to come here, we will fight him and chase him all the way back to Berlin."

Times were changing. Irene returned home for the summer to find neighbors renouncing their Polish heritage, speaking German. People openly admired Hitler's policies and embraced his leadership. Signs around town read, "Don't buy from Jews!"

Irene was saddened and confused. Never before had race and ethnicity been issues. She had many Jewish friends and couldn't imagine why such hatred existed. Living on the border of Germany, Irene felt Hitler's influence creeping into her neighborhood.

After Irene returned to nursing school, Radom's sky was full of bombers. War had begun. All of Irene's days and nights were spent at St. Mary's Hospital caring for the wounded.

They never had enough food, clean sheets, or medicine for everyone. Maimed Polish soldiers arrived in droves.

Irene had no way of knowing if her family was safe. She worked around the clock, dazed by the horrors around her. As the Germans continued to invade Radom, the Polish soldiers began to retreat and requested that doctors and nurses accompany their men in battle. Without reservation, Irene volunteered.

During those days, the streets were full of fleeing citizens. Houses were on fire. Wreckage and smoke were everywhere. Wounded soldiers covered the ground. Word came that Poland was no longer a country, and the Germans had seized Radom. The troops were in Russia, trying to stay alive.

One cold day, Irene was chosen to go on a bartering mission with four soldiers. Russian soldiers chased Irene, then beat and raped her. Police found her unconscious and took her to the hospital for medical help.

Irene was then a Soviet prisoner. She learned to speak Russian while being nursed back to health. But Irene didn't know what would happen to her, a renegade nurse from the Polish army. She cried out to God, feeling alone and defeated. With the help of a benevolent doctor, she finally escaped. After two long years, her prayers and courage finally led her home.

Irene's homecoming was sweet. Irene told her family all she had been through, and her father proudly said, "God has spared your life, and He has a plan for you." She was able to celebrate her nineteenth birthday with her family, though it was solemn. The Gut family barely had enough food to survive, but they managed to keep their faith and rely on their God. The war *had* to end soon.

One Sunday after morning worship, German soldiers were waiting outside the church. "You will be transported to Radom to work for the Reich," they said.

Irene's new work was packing ammunition boxes. Though she hated the drudgery, she was at least thankful to be in Radom again. The Germans soon discovered her fluency and decided she was better suited to work at an old, stately hotel. At the hotel, Irene was treated well. She served the German officials their meals and went about her domestic duties, often overhearing about the "Jewish problem." One day she witnessed a Hasidic Jew being brutally beaten outside the hotel window. She watched in horror. Herr Shulz, her boss, saw Irene's deep compassion for the man and warned her not to be a "Jew-lover." It was broadcasted over loudspeakers in the street: "Whoever helps a Jew shall be punished by death." But still she longed to help in some way.

Soon the city was Jew free except for the Jewish ghetto. During that time Irene's assignment changed once again. Herr Shulz loved Irene and trusted her, so she began to serve him as his housekeeper. Rokita, another German official, occasionally dined with Herr Shulz. Irene waited on them and overheard their plans and schemes for Hitler's regime. Thus she knew of the plans to completely rid the city of Jews.

Herr Shulz gave Irene a crew of workers from the nearby Jewish ghetto. The Jews who worked with her in the laundry room grew to trust her. Her conscience did not allow her to stand for the evils of the Third Reich, and Irene began scheming to find hiding for them.

One day, she found a vent in Herr Shulz's bathroom. Removing the grate, she saw that it could probably hold six people. It was perfect. No one would suspect that Herr Shulz would hide Jews. They stayed there until she could have them transported to a foxhole in the forest. She also hid her friends at a villa that Herr Shulz was having repaired. By then, everyone thought the city was *judenrein*—Jew-free—but Irene knew otherwise.

Irene ended up helping more than fifteen Jews escape death. She did not set out to be a hero. She merely knew she had to act—that God required it of her. He had faithfully watched over her and it was her turn to do the same for others. She never regretted her choice. She was simply thankful to be able to use her free will to rescue others.

* * *

Live such good lives among the pagans that, though they accuse you of doing wrong, they may see your good deeds and glorify God on the day he visits us.

(1 Peter 2:12)

WEEK NINE JOURNAL

———— ✦ ————

✦ What are you asking God to do in your life right now?

✦ When have you seen God answer your prayers in the past?

✦ If God were to answer your prayers, how would life be different?

✦ How can a Christian get her life in tune with God's plan?

✦ What Bible verse or passage of Scripture has been most meaningful to you this week? Why?

jessica corrill
ROCKING FOR LIFE

Three-year-old Jessica Corrill watched her father carrying boxes outside. She ran to the edge of the yard as he packed his belongings in the bed of his truck. After placing the last box carefully in the truck, he turned to look at his daughter. He picked her up and hugged her. "You didn't do anything wrong," he said, "but I have to go."

Afterward, Jessica's mom, racked by alcoholism, farmed her young daughter out to relatives and friends for days at a time. Eventually, Jessica was sent to Jackie and James Rhea's home, where she felt God's love for the first time. They took her to church.

At church, James Rhea was the children's pastor. He used puppets, music, and donuts to share Jesus Christ with the children gathered around him. "At my house," Jessica says, "Jesus had always been the baby in a manger that we set out for a month at Christmastime. Slowly, throughout the games and food and puppet shows, I started to catch on that Jesus was more than a baby in a manger. For some reason, Jesus loved me."

In first grade, Jessica heard the Easter story and gave her heart to Jesus. Her Sunday school teacher told her that Jesus loved her so much, He died for her. And He would never leave her. Later, during the adult service, the pastor invited people to come forward if they wanted to know Jesus. Jessica went.

"So many people say children get saved because they want to please others, not because they understand Jesus," Jessica reflects. "But when I went up to the altar that day at that little church on Columbia Street, I remember an instant change. I felt something different. I experienced the love of Christ."

When she went home that day, her mom asked, "So, how was church?"

"I got saved," Jessica said.

Her mom didn't say anything, just looked at her.

"I asked Jesus to be my Savior."

"Oh, that's nice," her mother said.

Soon, she began telling everyone about Jesus. On a chalkboard at home, Jessica wrote, "Mommy, I love you and Jesus does too. Will you go to church with me?"

Jessica could tell the message aggravated her mother. "Jesus isn't for me," she said.

In first grade, Jessica told her classmates about Jesus. "Have you been saved?" she asked.

Her best friend replied, "Well, a police officer pulled me out of a car wreck, so yeah, I've been saved." Jessica saw she needed to explain more about Jesus and heaven. Eventually she used the word *hell,* and her teacher reprimanded her.

Still, Jessica told her teacher, "God loves us all. Jesus died for our sins and if we tell Him we are sorry, we'll get to go to heaven, but if we don't tell Jesus we're sorry, we go to hell." The teacher lectured her about respecting other people's beliefs.

Adolescence brought more conflict. In Jessica's freshman year of high school, she was troubled by the movies her Spanish teacher showed in class—with language and situations inappropriate for a school setting. She told James Rhea what she had seen. He called the school board to point out the hypocrisy in having a rule about students' using vulgar language and teachers showing movies peppered with profanity.

The school board contacted the teacher. The teacher told her classes about Jessica and the school board. Her peers mocked Jessica, calling her a "sheltered Holy Roller." When she went into class one day, a girl muttered, "There goes that immature brat. She can't handle watching a movie because *God* might get upset."

In the hallways, Jessica caught bits of conversations meant for her ears. "There goes that Jesus freak who messes up everything," they said. "The problem with our school is girls like her."

Jessica never let it stop her. Today at sixteen, she has dedicated herself to a ministry called Rock for Life, the youth branch of the American Life League—the second largest pro-life organization in America. Rock for Life is committed to spreading the truth about abortion to today's emerging generation. Jessica distributes pro-life literature at malls. She's prayed in front of Planned Parenthood. She's penned poetry. One poem, entitled "The Unheard Voice," includes the following stanza:

What is abortion, Mommy? Can you tell me what it is?
I bet it's something good,
For you are my Mommy and Mommies do what is good.
Mommy, what is happening? What is going on?
Something is not right, Mommy. Something is very wrong.

Mommy, what is happening? They are taking me away.
Before they make me go, I just want to say
I love you very much and always remember me
For I will be with you in your memory.

"One third of my generation is gone—it really bothers me," Jessica explains. "It breaks my heart that in 1973 our country said it was all right to end life."

So Jessica has made a difference. As a leader in Rock for Life, Jessica sets up concerts that benefit right-to-life efforts. Pro-life bands sing for free, their concert income going directly to anti-abortion efforts nationwide.

Jessica wants to reach the girls of her generation. "There are so many young girls who feel helpless in their situations—as if there is only one choice," she says. "But there are so many others." Jessica states her mission this way: "When a baby is aborted, how does her message get out? It doesn't, because her voice is silenced. I will be a voice for the voiceless."

Jessica expresses God's love in her everyday actions, whether she is sharing Christ at school or protesting abortion. Although she faces jeering and ostracism as a sixteen-year-old, she sees these as opportunities to know God better: "When you begin to live the true life of a Christian, you will be persecuted and mocked. You will face hardships and trials. If life were perfect and I never had difficult times, how would I know what God could really do?"

Through it all, Jessica leans on the Father who never leaves. She remembers a conversation she had with a friend where she learned that one of the words Jesus used to describe the Father was *Abba,* which, loosely translated, means "Daddy."

"When I heard that, it hit me that God lets me come to Him and call him Daddy. He is there to pick me up and help me through anything. It amazes me."

Jessica is determined to listen to her Father's voice and act in His behalf—for all those who have no voice.

You received the Spirit of sonship. And by him we cry, "Abba, Father." The Spirit himself testifies with our spirit that we are God's children.

(Romans 8:15–16)

---

joy freed
BREAKING CHAINS

J ohn and Joy in the morning. Good morning to ya!" As the sun crests the prairie sky, Joy's laughter and warmth cross the vast open spaces of the Upper Midwest. Christian radio pulls in its listeners to share a common message, and Joy's is one of hope and encouragement. Here's a young woman who's made great sacrifice, yet few know her story of extraordinary strength and courage.

Joy wanted to believe the chain was broken the night her mother died. Her brilliant mom adored Joy. But bipolar disease, anxiety, panic disorders, failed marriages, lost careers, and ten years without a job made Joy's mom less than stable. Her life as a single mom came to an end with an overdose of heroin in a downtown hotel room in L.A. Joy was sixteen.

"She was my best friend," Joy says. "But she almost destroyed me. I will never love, hate, or miss anyone as much as my mother."

One year after her mom's death, Joy was living in San Paulo, Brazil, on a mission trip with two other American girls.

She thought distance would help her to leave the past behind. An outreach in a new and different country set the perfect stage where she could rewrite the script of her painful life. But was three thousand miles far enough from her mother's grave? How far did her chains reach?

Joy spent the next six months as a missionary working with homeless children, eating lots of rice, riding buses . . . and enjoying a tropical romance with a quiet man named Daniel. He was dark and beautiful, and one of the best drummers in the city. It was a shallow relationship, but those were Joy's favorite kind. Her mother had taught her well. All the young girl needed in a man was someone to reach out for in the dark when she felt alone. When Joy left Brazil, she and Daniel parted with a hug and a smile, and no plans of ever looking back.

But back in the U.S., two words changed her life forever. "You're pregnant," the doctor said during a routine exam. Joy was going to have a son. She named him Seth.

As it turns out, three thousand miles wasn't nearly far enough. Joy was still buried up to the neck in the results of her mother's bad choices, and now she had her own. Joy was nauseated—yes, from morning sickness, but really from the fact that she was repeating her mom's life. She decided that ruining her life was one thing, but ruining her son's was another. Adoption became a serious option.

With the help of a caring Christian adoption agency, Joy evaluated hundreds of families who might take her son. After she read about Darin and Shantel, she searched no more. They were a perfect fit. But for Joy, what lay ahead took far more courage than anything she'd ever encountered. One sleepless night she wrote in her journal:

PREGNANT. It's such a bulky, awkward word. Seven months into my pregnancy, I am feeling the same way. It's disturbing to watch life approach a corner knowing that whatever lies on the other side will change me forever.

And although it could, should, and will destroy me, a part of me wonders if it won't perhaps save me as well—from myself, from the person I seemed destined to become.

When I stop and try to turn in the other direction, life unmercifully pushes me forward. Tiny feet kick against my ribs, unrelenting. One day the restless life inside will be gone. So I close my eyes and brace myself for the storms of grief, separation, and heartbreak.

But inside, I clutch the warm memory of a tiny hand pushing against my tummy, of a heart beating in time with mine, and of nine glorious months of companionship and sorrow. My body will never forget and my mind will always remember. And so, gripping these memories, one foot in front of the other, I walk on, preparing to give away a part of my soul.

Joy was not prepared for the way she would love her first child—or for the pain of giving up that child. In no hurry, Seth showed up two weeks late and landed in the doctor's hands with a vengeance. At ten pounds, two ounces, he was huge, beautiful, and absolutely perfect.

Ten minutes after he was born, Joy put him in the arms of his new mom. They both cried because Joy couldn't be his mom, and they both cried because Shantel could. Joy stayed with Seth in the hospital for three days, her only time as his mother outside the womb—the three most precious days of Joy's life.

That was almost three years ago. Some nights Joy wakes up and feels as if she's just come home from the hospital. Mostly the memories come to her in flashes at random, unguarded times. A glimpse of his hand curled around hers hits when she's at work. Love and heartbreak are sewn together inside her now, wrapped around her few memories as a mother. She can never have one without the other.

The hardest moments come when Joy thinks not of what was, but of what could have been. Her mind jumps forward, and suddenly it's her holding Seth's hand as they walk through the park, her watching Seth run, her swinging him around and picking him up in the way only a mother can. The vision that tortures her most is their walking together and his calling her "Mom," looking at her with his big, happy brown eyes.

Not every woman's situation is right for adoption. Despite her pain, Joy insists hers was. "Adoption is never about feeling good," she says. "It's about choosing something that nearly kills you for the betterment of someone else's life. The day I let Seth go, something inside of me died. But with that death, the chain was broken, and I realized I had done the one thing my mother never could do. In my sacrifice, I had chosen for my son a better life."

Joy understands now what it cost God to stand back and watch the end of His Son's sinless life while He cried for his Father. She understands the price Jesus paid that she might become His daughter. She understands what it cost God to love Joy enough to let her walk away from Him. But most of all, she knows what it cost Him to swing her around and pick her up (as only a Father can) when she came running back to Him, dragging her broken chains, calling Him "Dad," and looking up at Him with her big, happy brown eyes.

*I will not sacrifice to the L*ORD *my God burnt offerings that cost me nothing.*

(2 Samuel 24:24)

rebecca

PROMISE OF PEACE

A slender young woman walked through the door and plopped down on the couch. Cara had been anxiously waiting for her to arrive. Sitting across from her visitor, Cara ran her finger over the spirals of the notebook next to her. She felt nervous about how to begin. The visitor, however, seemed confident and enveloped with a startling sense of peace.

The hum of the fan filled the room. The two women had met for a special purpose. The visitor, Rebecca, had a story to tell—one she claimed the hand of the Master Author Himself had written. "Where would you like me to begin?" she asked.

Cara pulled her legs up on the couch, using them as a writing surface for her notebook. "However you feel led is fine," she said.

"Well . . . I grew up in an awesome family. We kissed, hugged, and laughed all the time." Her face softened. "Every Sunday, when I was little, Mom helped me dress and fix my hair. Then all five of us would scramble into the car for church. Christianity for Mom and Dad was more of a family tradition than a meaningful relationship with God. The only day the Christian life impacted them was Sunday. Then when I grew older, life got busy and we just stopped going altogether.

"In high school I met some really neat friends. They invited me to Fellowship of Christian Athletes. A few months later I volunteered to help organize an outreach event. On the day of the event, I sat in the audience listening to students give their testimonies. It was then that I realized I didn't have one. *Could God give me my own personal story to share?* I wondered. I knew Bible stories and that God loved me, but I was empty.

"That night I gave my life to God. Immediately, I started praying for Mom and Dad and felt compelled to sit down and explain the gospel to them. I was surprised when they were in agreement with everything I shared."

Rebecca stopped to let Cara catch up. Cara glanced over her notes and turned to a fresh page, then nodded for Rebecca to continue. The testament of God's love in Rebecca's life had just begun. The next chapter of her story began to unfold in the mountains of Montana.

Rebecca plunged her nose into the scented pillow. She snuggled down in the twin bed under a heavy quilt. The smell of the cabin filled her senses. She breathed in, letting memories of giggling carry her toward sleep. She had always loved the mountain cabin where her family vacationed and was glad to be back even if Kristen, her oldest sister, hadn't been able to come. Her mom, dad, and sister Kate were there and in the morning they would all go skiing. They would come back tired, cold, and very happy. Fresh powder makes for the best skiing, and that year there was lots of it. Rebecca rolled over and saw that Kate was already asleep. Soon she would drift off too.

She woke startled. Her father stood at the foot of the bed, shaking her feet. *Oh no, I overslept and missed the chance to make first tracks!* But then her father's frantic voice filled her ears. "Get up, get up! You need to get out of the cabin right now! Get up, Rebecca! There's a fire! Get up!" She watched him as he ran across the room to open the bedroom window. His voice was strong. "Come on, girls, through the window, right now!" He eased Rebecca, then Kate out the window into the snow. They were safe. Shaken but relieved, Rebecca gulped in the freezing air.

Did the dogs make it out? Panic gripped Rebecca's mind. Barefooted, she ran through the snow calling out into the cold night. "MacKenzie! Hunter!" Kate joined in, "Hunter! MacKenzie!" The girls' cries floated into the air.

Rebecca turned as flames leapt from the cabin, lighting the blackness. No sign of the dogs and . . . no sign of her parents. Her feet burned with cold and her eyes stung from the heavy smoke. "Where are they?" she screamed to Kate. "Where are Mom and Dad?"

She didn't remember hearing her father's feet hit the ground below the window. His voice had not called out for the dogs. He must have turned back for their mother. On feet they could no longer feel, Rebecca and Kate ran to the front of the cabin. Physical shock had taken over and Rebecca plunged her hands, unfeeling, into the snow for rocks. Kate smashed them through window after window. "Mom! Dad!" The only response was the roar of flames.

Rebecca shifted her weight on the couch, glancing at the floor while she drew a deep breath. Her eyes met Cara's. Cara's pen shook slightly.

"I prayed the entire time," Rebecca finally said. "I prayed over and over again, 'Lord, let them find a way out!' I don't know the passage of time, but eventually I found myself saying instead, 'I know they are with You. Thank You.'

"The days that followed were incredibly hard—beyond description, really. But I clung to God's Word. I read His promises over and over. Somehow, in the midst of all the tragedy, deep in my spirit I knew He would redeem all the pain and make it good for His kingdom. Somehow I knew even then that He would give me peace and lasting purpose."

As the snow melted into warm spring days, Rebecca said, the riverbeds filled with rushing waters. Summer emerged and the river cleared and ran like glass in the mountain streams of Montana. One day, Rebecca settled down on the bank of the Stillwater River and considered the passing seasons of her own life—how winter had blown in tragedy and the spring thaw had made grief swell within her like bulging riverbanks raging with runoff from the melted snow. But now the summer sun warmed her back, and she poured out her thanks to God: "Father, You have been my refuge and my strength. Even in troubled waters, You have comforted me."

As she prayed, the peace of God embraced her and for the first time in many seasons, she felt her joy return. She knew well the words of the psalmist and made them her own: "God, you are my 'refuge and strength, / [my] ever-present help in trouble'. . . . You, Lord Almighty, are with me" [Ps. 46:1,11]. This is *my* story, Lord. Truly You have sustained me in peace. I trust You will show me when to share it."

Less than a year after the fire, God gave Rebecca an opportunity to share the story she had not chosen but had received with a promise. Twenty people were saved that day. Rebecca continues to write and share her story with those who need to hear.

Cara closed her notebook. The purr of the fan filled the air, and the two women sat together in silence for another moment. Cara had intended only to write Rebecca's story, but as Rebecca left the room, she left the gift of peace with yet one more who needed to hear.

————————————————————————

Therefore we will not fear,
    though the earth give way
and the mountains fall into the heart of the sea,
    though its waters roar and foam
and the mountains quake with their surging.

(Psalm 46:2–3)

————————————————————————

bonnie witherall
ORDINARY GIRL, EXTRAORDINARY GOD

Bonnie Penner was a normal teenager who sometimes argued with her mother when it was time to get ready for school and loved to play with the family dog, Lady. Yet Bonnie had a desire to help those in need and a passion for sharing the love of Jesus that would take her to three continents and eventually to heaven.

"She was an ordinary girl with a desire to share the gospel," remembers her mother, Ann. When Bonnie was fourteen, she left her hometown of Vancouver, Washington, to go on her first short-term mission project. A few short weeks in Florida at a Teen Missions boot camp solidified Bonnie's passion for ministry. Throughout her high-school years, Bonnie participated in outreach projects for the homeless in Portland, Oregon, went to England and Mexico for summer mission trips, and led her fellow McDonald's employees in prayer before their shifts.

After high school, Bonnie attended Bible school in Germany. God continued to draw her to people with physical needs, and after she returned to Washington, Bonnie enrolled in nursing school. It quickly became clear that her concerns were more spiritual than physical, so when she was twenty-two years old, Bonnie transferred to Moody Bible Institute in Chicago, where she majored in missions. She continued to travel the world on short-term missions, including a six-week trip to the Philippines.

Bonnie's passion for Christ shone in every area of her life. The father of children she babysat while she was at Moody wrote to her parents:

> When Bonnie returned from the Philippines, she told us about her experiences and the work she had done there. From the perspective of our comfortable life, it was clear that she had lived without all the conveniences we are accustomed to here. Hearing her stories, I wondered if she had been frustrated by any of the challenges she faced. Bonnie replied quickly and simply, almost in a matter-of-fact way, "No, because He wanted me to be there." In that moment and simple phrase, I saw pure faith in God and love for Him and His people shine brilliantly in your daughter.

In the midst of her busy schedule, Bonnie met fellow student Gary Witherall. Bonnie had dated occasionally during high school and at Moody, but no one had ever captured her heart. She told her mother that she was hesitant to fall in love, afraid someone would come into her life who would keep her from what God wanted her to do. But in Gary, she met a man whose passion for missions rivaled her own. It was love at first sight, and the two married just after graduation.

Bonnie and Gary moved to Portland, Oregon, and began to look for ways to serve God overseas. When their first assignment choice fell through, Bonnie was disappointed but determined. "I have come to realize that God has not called me to a place," she told Gary. "He has called me to Himself."

Not long afterward, Bonnie and Gary were accepted by Operation Mobilization and assigned to southern Lebanon in January 2001. Her sister Cheryl told *The Oregonian* newspaper that the family was concerned, but supportive. "Bonnie was doing exactly what she wanted to do. She said, 'I've found my niche in the world.' I think that she found true happiness, and she wanted to share that with other people."

Bonnie and Gary settled in Sidon, a city mentioned often in the Bible, for two years of language training. In Lebanon, Bonnie discovered a people in desperate need of both the love of Christ and the physical comfort she felt called to provide. She began volunteering at the Unity Center, a Christian prenatal clinic for Palestinian women living in the poverty-stricken Ain al-Hiweh refugee camp. Acting both as an administrator and an assistant, Bonnie interacted with clinic patients every day. She helped deliver babies, offered clothing and supplies, and answered any questions the refugee women had. She built relationships with the women, and if they asked her about her reasons, she gave them Bibles and talked to them about her faith in Jesus.

Bonnie loved what she was doing and cared deeply about the women she served. In an e-mail to her former pastor, Bonnie wrote, "I feel this overwhelming joy in being here. I have such a heart for the women in this camp and I can touch their lives through the clinic."

Friends and coworkers say that Bonnie tried to avoid the political upheaval that was happening around her. Local Muslim leaders began to condemn the clinic staff for sharing the message of Christ and converting local Muslims. The clinic and associated church received threats. Yet Bonnie remained committed to her work. If talk turned to politics, her coworkers said, Bonnie changed the subject. She would rather talk about people and relationships, and how better to serve the women in the clinic.

In an interview with the *New York Times*, Sidon's Roman Catholic archbishop George Kwaiter said, "We told her she might be vulnerable to insults or even being hit, and she answered that she would consider it an honor."

Even after the terrorist attacks in America on September 11, 2001, Bonnie overcame her fear and continued to serve. "What is there to be afraid of?" she asked her mother while they chatted online one day. When friends visited Bonnie and Gary, she told them, "I wish every believer could enjoy her ministry so much that she wouldn't want to be anywhere else."

On the morning of November 21, 2002, Bonnie arrived at the Unity Center at eight o'clock, as usual. Waiting for her outside was a single gunman. When Bonnie opened the clinic's front door, he shot her three times at point-blank range. Bonnie Penner Witherall died instantly.

As Gary accompanied his wife's body from Lebanon to the United States, he struggled with his grief. Eventually, though, he found peace in the same calling that had drawn his wife to Lebanon in the first place. In the many memorial services that followed the death of this compassionate, faith-filled woman, Gary spoke out again and again about forgiveness. "You either hate and be angry, or you forgive. I have to forgive."

Their message of Jesus' death and resurrection was worth the price that they paid. "God led us to Lebanon and we knew that we might die," Gary told *The Times* of London. "It's a costly forgiveness. . . . It cost my wife."

Letters poured in to Bonnie's parents and to Gary. People

they never met—from elementary schoolteachers to former coworkers—shared stories of how Bonnie had touched their lives.

Gary's voice broke often during the memorial services for Bonnie, but at one point, he shouted as he proclaimed, "So many people think [Bonnie's] death was a waste . . . but we believed that coming here with the message of Jesus would never be a waste. . . . I will take this message as long as I live. The tomb's empty! Bonnie is dancing with Jesus!"

This is the testimony: God has given us eternal life, and this life is in His Son. He who has the Son has life. He who does not have the Son does not have life. I write these things to you who believe in the name of the Son of God so that you may know that you have eternal life.

(1 John 5:11–13)

brittany hamilton
CONFIDENCE IN GOD

Brittany Hamilton accepted Christ when she was seven years old, but she never dreamed she would need to lean on the Lord so severely in the early years of her faith.

On October 25, 1994, when Brittany was nine, she waited for her mother to pick her up from school. Kathleen Hamilton was always on time. Brittany waited and waited, knowing in her gut that something was terribly wrong. Her parents had driven out together that morning, looking for a good spot to hunt deer for an upcoming hunting trip. But they should have been back in time to pick her up. At 5:30, the secretary from Brittany's church picked her up and took her to see her pastor.

"Your parents have been in a train accident, Brittany, and your mom went to be with the Lord." Brittany remembers crying but not fully understanding. Pastor Frank then took her to the hospital where her dad was in a coma and not expected to live more than four or five days. Everyone who cared for Brittany was there to comfort her. But nothing seemed real. In just a matter of minutes, Brittany lost her loving mother and faced the reality that she might lose her dad as well.

Miraculously, Gary Hamilton survived. But Brittany soon learned that her father was paralyzed. No more playing outside with Dad. No more walks together. And because he had to endure many months of rehab, Brittany would have to wait to feel the warmth of her father's hugs.

Brittany finally moved into the hospital quarters so she didn't have to be separated from her dad anymore. She saw some of the difficult, painful medical procedures that her father had to undergo. The therapist often just pushed him out of his wheelchair to see how he coped. She hated how they treated him.

When she became discouraged, Gary reminded his daughter that some in the hospital were even worse off than he was. Some had no feeling at all and couldn't ever hug their children again. He had the blessing of being able to use his limbs and hold Brittany on his lap. The bond between them grew through the struggles, and God knitted their hearts together for His purposes.

Gary felt Brittany needed some time away from the hospital. Her aunt and uncle had a ranch in Wyoming, and they invited her to come visit for the summer. They had horses and Brittany learned to ride. She fell in love with the sport and enjoyed the beauty of the outdoors. "I think God gave me horses so I would be less focused on the loss of my mother," she says. "I could ride for hours looking over the vast canyon all around me. I just let the beauty minister to me, and I bonded with my horse. My horse listened to me cry, yell, and scream. I was angry, sad, and all those things you would expect. It's amazing, but horses really do listen. Their ears flicker, letting you know they hear you. My horse was a much-needed companion."

Today, Brittany is nineteen years old. She now has three horses and competes in local rodeo events. Trophies line her living-room shelves, attesting to her strong will and dedication. The proud owner of Snazzy, a grand champion, Brittany also has aspirations to compete for Miss Rodeo America.

Most of her events are on Sundays, but she is able to participate in Christian ministries for those on the rodeo circuit. "My dad has reminded me that even though it is difficult to miss church, I can still share my faith with others," she says. "God has promised us that wherever two or three are gathered, there He is in our midst." Brittany is involved with a program called Women Behind Cowboys, which encourages young girls to stay in the Word and to run the real race, which is for Christ.

Brittany also has completed a CNA (Certified Nursing Assistant) program and is working at her local hospital. "I saw how some of the medical staff treated my dad, and I decided I want to spend my life caring for people." Brittany plans to attend the University of Wyoming to further study nursing and equine nutrition.

Many of the whys of the accident are still puzzling. The engineer operating the train was not at the front of the train when the Hamiltons' car was hit. He didn't see them coming, and then it was too late to stop. Why did God allow man's carelessness to have such a devastating outcome? What if the Hamiltons had come along just a few minutes earlier? God could have spared Brittany from loss and grief. Why would a loving God allow this to happen to a young girl?

With a humble disposition, Brittany admits that it has been very hard to accept everything, and she still struggles with the effects of the accident on her life.

"I still miss my mom. To me, she was an angel. I remember she was good to everyone she met. She always was upbeat, and I never wanted to leave her side. Yes, I would love to have my mom back, but I know I wouldn't be who I am and who God has made me to be.

"I still struggle with why it had to happen, but I've learned God will never give me more than I can handle. I could have chosen to hate God and could be living apart from God's best for me. But for some reason, God has blessed me and chosen to entrust me with the great responsibility of caring for my dad."

Brittany admits that many of her friends have not understood the weight of her responsibilities. Her schedule does not look like that of a typical teenager because she has to run her home: wash laundry, cook, and clean. She makes it a priority to be home by 10:30 to tend to her dad's medical needs. She has lost friends who get tired of Brittany's demanding schedule. With conviction, Brittany has always told them, "Sorry, my dad is more important than bowling."

Though the struggles continue, Brittany's faith is strong and real. "The accident has given me the opportunity to find strength and confidence I would not have known otherwise. When my dad and I are out together at horse shows, we share our faith. People see the bond between us. And we know, without the Lord, we wouldn't be here together."

The LORD is my shepherd, I shall not be in want.
He makes me lie down in green pastures,
he leads me beside quiet waters,
he restores my soul.

WEEK TEN JOURNAL

+= What areas of your life would you like to see changed?

+= How can someone surrender difficult areas of her life to God?

+= If you were to surrender completely to Him, how would you know that God will take care of you, no matter what happens?

+= In your view, what is a costly sacrifice? Why would someone make a sacrifice like that?

+= What Bible verse or passage of Scripture has been most meaningful to you this week? Why?

purnima

FAITH DESPITE SORROW

When only thirteen, Purnima found herself having to say good-bye to her parents. She had professed her faith in Christ, and officials demanded she either denounce her faith or leave Bhutan. She knew she could not deny Christ. He was the only one who could save her.

The officers interrogated Purnima and thirty-four other believers, asking the same questions over and over. "Why do you want to be a Christian? This is a Buddhist country, and you have dishonored us by accepting this foreign religion." She and the others were given five days to leave their homes and go to Nepal. Christians were labeled "traitors," and the other villagers openly attacked them.

A year before, Purnima's parents had forced her out of their home. Purnima was the daughter of a witch doctor, who led the village in rituals and performed animal sacrifices to drive out evil spirits. Her older sister, Maya, had suffered a serious illness, and she watched her father perform Buddhist rituals and sacrifice chickens for three years, calling on the spirits to heal his daughter. It never worked. Purnima could not understand why nothing her father did appeased the gods.

Miraculously, Maya was healed, but not through the incantations of a witch doctor. Maya claimed that Jesus had healed her. Maya's husband, Sival, had a Bible and they had prayed for Jesus to heal her. Purnima's father was so enraged at such a claim, he kicked Maya and Sival out of the home. Their newfound faith was a disgrace to the family. Purnima was heartbroken when they left, and no one was allowed to mention Maya in the home.

Soon, there was news that Sival and Maya had a baby boy. Purnima knew they lived outside the village and couldn't keep away from her sister any longer. She had to go meet her nephew! Her curiosity about Maya's new faith remained. What kind of God would just heal, asking nothing in return? How did Sival and Maya have such strength to stand against their families and leave Buddhism?

Purnima cut across fields, hiding in the brush so she could remain out of sight. When Maya opened the door to their small hut, she embraced her little sister with joy. The visits continued, and Maya began reading stories from the Bible to her sister. Purnima was fascinated with the story of Moses. He left his home to become a mouthpiece for God. She wondered what God would have her do if she were a Christian.

Finally, Purnima's mother confronted her. "We know what you are doing. I've lost one daughter, and I don't want to lose another. Do you understand?" Her mother explained how Christianity was for a lower class of people and not acceptable to their family or their country. But Purnima couldn't keep away from her sister. She kept visiting and hearing more about Jesus.

That Christmas, Sival and Maya invited her over for a small celebration. There, she accepted Jesus as Savior and wanted to be baptized.

Maya was overjoyed for her sister but also feared what might happen to her. At first, she thought it might be best for Purnima to keep her faith to herself and not tell her parents. But Purnima knew she could never hide it. It was too real. Maya offered to go with her, but her little sister was determined to do it alone. She walked home and blurted out, "Mom, I'm a Christian." Her mother thought she was joking but soon realized it was true. That evening, her parents forced her to leave home.

As she began her journey, she could hear her mother crying. Purnima knew her mother really did still love her. She lived with Maya and Sival until the arrests of Christians began. But then she had to prepare to leave Bhutan.

She wanted to see her parents just one more time. She quietly opened her front door. "Mom? Mom, it's me." Her mother grabbed her and tears flowed as she held her tightly. "Please tell me you are not a Christian any longer." Purnima was silent for a while and finally knew she had to tell her she was leaving Bhutan. Her mother looked at her, asking, "How can you be so brave? You are so young and innocent." Her father entered the room, giving her a roll of money. He told her to be careful and quietly left.

Purnima stayed a few more minutes, desperately trying to memorize her mother's face. She didn't know if she would gaze into her eyes or hear her sweet voice again. They embraced one last time and Purnima slipped into the dark night, darting through the familiar fields one last time.

In the morning, she joined eight other believers who were also being forced to leave. They got on a bus and were dropped off near the border. There would be no more contact with home. Making their way toward Nepal, they journeyed sorrowfully, crying silent tears. Purnima cried herself to sleep each night, thinking of her village and her family. Every night she had vivid dreams of her mother. She just wanted to be her little girl again.

One night she was awakened by a heavy boot slamming into her side. She didn't know how many bandits were attacking them, but her small group did not resist. The men had guns and lined them up, ordering them to close their eyes. They obeyed, wondering if they would be shot. Finally, they opened their eyes to find the gunmen had left, stealing all they had. Everyone had lost all his or her money, except Purnima. She had hidden the money her father gave her very well.

The next morning, they were able to get a ride to Nepal with Purnima's money. The group was thankful for the young girl's bravery and wit. The group used the ride to catch up on sleep. Purnima was thankful the thieves had not taken her Bible. She read about Joseph and Mary fleeing to Egypt, giving her courage to face another day on the run.

The truck stopped to refuel, so everyone got out to walk and stretch. They ran into a pastor and shared their story. The pastor was particularly sympathetic to young Purnima. He asked her companions if he could invite her to live with his family. Purnima was grateful but she still missed her family desperately.

A few months later, the pastor took her to a Christian conference. She was elated to see Sival! Now she could live with her sister. The pastor tried to convince Purnima to stay with him, knowing she would end up living in a refugee camp. Purnima understood that what he said was true but wanted to be with family more than anything. Sival led his sister-in-law to their camp on the northern border. There the sisters were reunited, shrieking with joy.

While Purnima loved being with Maya and Sival, she hated the conditions of the camp. Despair seemed to be all around. Thousands of families were living in severe poverty. But Maya assured her that they could make a difference and share Jesus with the refugees. Purnima began sharing her faith with others, soon forgetting the deplorable living situation.

She couldn't help it. Purnima knew the rules of the camp, but she had to share the love of Jesus. Purnima soon found herself occupying a prison cell for spreading her faith in Nepal. Even in the lowest pit, which seemed like hell itself, this young brave girl brought others to Christ. She was released after fourteen months and sixteen days, and she still lives with Maya and Sival, hoping one day to share the gospel with her mother.

So young, so experienced in serving and suffering for Christ: Purnima has proven that no cost is too great. She gladly gives all for her faith, despite her sorrow.

Finally, be strong in the Lord and in his mighty power. Put on the full armor of God so that you can take your stand against the devil's schemes.

(Ephesians 6:10–11)

---

amanda purcell
OBEYING WHEN IT HURTS

Amanda Marie Purcell grew up in a home where God was honored and loved. She prayed to receive Jesus in elementary school. "From that point on," she said, "it was my choice, not my parents, that persuaded me to follow God."

It was in the throes of adolescence that she felt His nearness in a unique way. During her junior year of high school, Amanda started dating a guy she'd known since eighth grade. Even though this boy had once run with a bad crowd, he apparently had turned his life around. Amanda felt drawn to him, particularly because he seemed needy. "We began talking, and we hit it off really well and ended up going out. Our relationship was always fun, extremely simple," she says. "We even prayed together and read Christian books."

But there was a problem: his anger. It prevented him from progressing in his walk with Jesus, and Amanda could see it. "I was in a relationship with an awesome guy—he was fun, good-looking, and loved Jesus. Our personalities fit well together, but at the same time he wasn't moving forward in knowing Jesus more. His anger would get the best of him.

Instead of my moving forward in my walk with Christ, I was using all my forward momentum to bring him up to my level."

One weekend, Amanda sensed it was time to break up. "No one ever came up to me and suggested it. It was just a God moment where I *knew* He was talking to me."

She broke up with the boy two days shy of their dating six months. "I can't explain the grief I felt at that moment," she says. "I wasn't breaking up with him because I didn't like him. I wasn't breaking up with him because he was mean to me. He never took his anger out on me. He treated me like a princess. The *only* reason I broke up with him was that God was telling me to."

After a year of grieving—crying every day for three months, and off and on for nine more—Amanda realized how glad she was that she made the choice to obey God. There were times during that year that her heart grew cold toward the Lord. "Sometimes I wondered why God had me break up with him. I couldn't see how it was helping me. I thought I had broken up with him so I could grow closer to God, but I felt farther from Him than ever before because my heart was so focused on the loss."

She realizes today where her life would be if she had kept dating the boy. "I would be thousands of steps behind where I was then if I were still with him now," she said. "I praise God that He gave me enough strength to get through that time."

Amanda now spends her time working with inner-city kids in the Eugene, Oregon, area. She started a dance group at her home church. Along with several other leaders, Amanda teaches kids how to dance for Jesus. They perform once a month and have a short Bible study each week after practice. Amanda has seen several kids grow in their relationships with God.

Even in the midst of serving Jesus, loving kids who need Him and glorifying Him through the arts, Amanda has had to learn to dig deeper in her faith. Instead of ministry driving her to the feet of Jesus, she got wrapped up in the excitement of ministry—of reaching kids. "I began to do it for the kids. I did it so we could have another cool ministry."

Eventually she came to see how important it was to serve Jesus for His sake and glory, not for her own, not for a sense of accomplishment. Amanda asked herself some tough questions. *Is this ministry good? Do I love Jesus with my whole heart?* "Yes and yes," she answered. "But was I tithing my time and efforts to the right thing? No. I was not doing it for the sole purpose of praising God."

She came to the place where she wanted only Jesus. "That's my prayer," she said. "I always want to be seeking Jesus, sitting at His feet, knowing and loving Him more."

That desire to be with Jesus translates into Amanda's actions on behalf of others. One day she saw a girl she didn't know at church who seemed distant and sullen. Amanda spent time with her, asking lots of questions. Ellie was homeless, living in a tent where her parents sold meth. "When it was time for her to leave, I was broken," Amanda said. "I had no way to contact her. I didn't know if I would ever see her again."

But over the next few months, Ellie came to church again and again. Amanda sought her out. "I was always fascinated at how much she could talk. I sat and listened to her stories and dropped snippets of godly advice whenever possible.

"But she had a hard time leaving her life behind her," Amanda says. "She didn't enjoy most Christians because of their rules, and she couldn't understand why people would choose a pure lifestyle. But for some reason, I found favor in her eyes."

Ellie continued to go to church for a year as her friendship with Amanda deepened. Amanda noticed that whenever worship began at church, Ellie started crying. One Sunday afternoon, when they were on their way to Amanda's house, Ellie seemed ready to meet Jesus. "We pulled over into an empty school parking lot in my little beat-up '88 Honda and got down to business," Amanda says.

Ellie met Christ in the abandoned parking lot. "It was funny because I always thought it would be this huge emotional experience, but it wasn't really," Amanda says. "There was a firmness and solitude about it. She had finally come home to the one who loves her most. And in that, we became bonded in the name of Jesus Christ as sisters. We still hang out to this day." Around church, Amanda calls Ellie "NC"—for New Creation.

Amanda is currently working part-time in her church with youth and trusting God to provide for her needs. She says, "It is exciting to get a glimpse of what my future will be like when I constantly put it in God's hands. But it's not even about the future, or the outcome. It's about the here and now. It's about the process of each moment. God is teaching me to walk in the Holy Spirit all the time."

Even when it hurts.

Jesus [said], "I am the way and the truth and the life. No one comes to the Father except through me."

(John 14:6)

---

ling

WILLING TO SUFFER

It was 1973 and nine-year-old Ling watched her father die of cancer, wondering if there really was a God at all. Ling and her family lived in a tiny bamboo hut in China. They had always been poor, unsure of when the next meal would come. Once her father had passed away, surviving was even more difficult.

Ling's mother and father had been inseparable. They never exchanged harsh words. The children saw their deep love for each other and for God. Ling knew her mother was deeply distraught at losing her husband, but nothing seemed to shake her faith in God.

Winter was setting in and the hut was cold. Ling's mother asked her to kneel down and pray with her one morning. Ling resented the request, as she really couldn't see any evidence that God cared for them. Her mother continued to pour out her heart to God with great fervor. Ling just knelt quietly, not wanting to say anything to God, even if He did exist.

Ling's mother realized that they would not be able to survive financially. She told the children that the family needed to move in with their grandmother. In Chinese culture, women depended on men for their well-being and happiness, but Ling's mother was not interested in remarrying. She wanted to go to work and get a job. Her mother was very opposed to the idea.

After two years, Ling's grandmother announced that she had arranged another marriage for her mother. "Mother, I don't want to marry again. I could never love anyone the way I loved Jun." Her mother's pleading did no good, and she had to heed her parent's wishes. Ling and her siblings had to adjust to a new stepfather.

Shu-tan did not treat the children well. Ling despised him but kept her feelings to herself. She was strong and healthy and began working as soon as she was allowed. In the fields she earned almost as much as any man. She also helped design a machine that made tofu. At fifteen, she desperately wanted to get away from her stepfather.

Ling didn't hear her mother pray as often as she once did. The prayers she did overhear occasionally were for Ling and her sister, who labored many hours under Shu-tan's orders. Her mother was one of the few secret believers in the village of Ru Tain. Disdain grew stronger each day between Shu-tan and Ling. Finally, he suggested she find a husband. He didn't care for her and wanted one less mouth to feed.

Ling continued to work harder and harder, avoiding her stepfather's path. He didn't press the idea of marriage. Ling was grateful and just kept working all she could. Work took her mind off her family's situation. She knew her mother was not happy, but she knew she could not change Shu-tan.

But one day, Ling saw her mother beam with a hope she had not seen in some time. Her mother excitedly told her an evangelist was coming to the village. All Ling felt toward God was bitterness, but to please her mother, Ling attended the evangelist's meeting.

While the evangelist preached, Ling felt her heart soften and she began to listen intently. Though she had heard the gospel before, it had never made sense to her. But that night was different. Her heart was stirred and she knew God was real. She wept, realizing the pain she had caused her mother, mocking her prayers and rejecting her faith. Ling's mother embraced her, offering forgiveness and assurance that God had a plan for her life.

For the next year, Ling attended Bible meetings with her mother. Her outlook changed, and she felt joy in her life for the first time. Then she began to have dreams about wheat fields. She didn't know what they meant, until at a prayer meeting, Ling and her mother read Luke 10: "The harvest is plentiful, but the workers are few" (v. 2). Ling knew God was calling her to preach the gospel. Her mother knew it was time for her to obey God's call.

At seventeen, with little money and no Bible, Ling set out to preach to the lost souls of China. She walked from village to village, sharing her faith. Some of the villages she visited had a Bible, so she studied and tried to memorize Scripture when she could. Ling preached with charisma and conviction, and young people particularly were drawn to her ministry. The people of China were starved for a message of hope.

Ling's ministry continued to grow. Hundreds gathered to hear her preach and share her faith. Many house churches formed in the villages, and the government began to take notice. Ling was put on the "most wanted" list. Her life on the run began.

For a while, she was able to keep running, sharing the gospel wherever she went, but finally officials threw her into prison. She became very ill but continued to labor with the other prisoners. Officers beat her at her interrogation, but she never gave them the answers they wanted. Finally, after five months of brutal treatment, they had to admit they had no evidence that she had done anything wrong. Reluctantly, they let her go.

Ling enjoyed her freedom and continued to preach and encourage the house churches. Later, she faced prison once again. She suffered severe loneliness, illness, and hardships of every kind. But whenever possible, she shared her trials and challenged the crowds to live for Christ, no matter the cost.

Life on the run hasn't gotten easier for Ling. But she is well educated in the school of suffering and knows danger will always loom over her path. The house churches of China continue to grow because of faithful believers like Ling. Two-thirds of the evangelistic teams sent to remote villages were women during the early stages of this movement. Who would have thought God could use a skeptical, bitter young girl to bring hope to the villages of China?

Ling's ministry continues today, as she continues to look for opportunities to plant more house churches. Imprisonment, illness, hunger, and persecution seem inevitable, but Ling remains resolved to take on the dangerous work of evangelism. She is willing to suffer because she knows the cause is worthy.

I know what it is to be in need, and I know what it is to have plenty. I have learned the secret of being content in any and every situation, whether well fed or hungry, whether living in plenty or in want.

(Philippians 4:12)

---

vicki

GROWING IN JESUS

Vicki always wanted to be a mom and have a family when she grew up. Her childhood was a hard one, and there wasn't much time for the fun and play other children enjoyed. Vicki's father was an alcoholic and suffered from emphysema. Money was tight, and fighting and stress filled her home.

At an early age, Vicki learned to help her mother with the household duties and bought her own clothes. She spent many hours in the hospital visiting her dad. The emphysema was killing him. Though her dad wouldn't stop drinking, he wanted his children to learn to love the Lord. Vicki went to church every Sunday and at an early age made a decision to follow Christ. Despite all the struggles in her home, she knew that Jesus brought hope.

At seventeen, Vicki started dating Gary. They met at the bowling alley where he worked. Though he was not a Christian, she was quickly drawn to his kind, gentle spirit. His demeanor was so attractive, so different, from the strife she had experienced at home. The young couple soon found themselves in love. Vicki and Gary were inseparable.

As a Christian, she knew she should abstain from sex until marriage. But six months into the relationship, Vicki found herself pregnant.

Marriage was the only option Vicki and Gary considered. Vicki had always wanted a baby girl, but she knew this wasn't the way to start a family. She had fallen short of God's best for her. How could she tell her father? Her sister had become pregnant out of wedlock, but she knew her parents expected better from Vicki. And the families at church—what would they think? Vicki feared rejection and judgment. She desperately wanted her Christian family to love her baby despite her mistake. Through all the complications, Gary and Vicki planned their wedding and were anxious for the birth of their baby.

The pregnancy was difficult. Vicki was very sick. Surprisingly, everyone supported Gary and Vicki in the months ahead. Her church threw them a beautiful baby shower, providing all she would need as a new mother. Cristina Marie was born June 20, 1970. Vicki couldn't believe how beautiful she was. God had blessed them with a baby girl, and the doctor said she was perfectly healthy! Life was looking up for the young couple despite the rough beginning.

Vicki loved being a mother and doted on her daughter. But after several months, Cristina became sick. Vicki took her to the doctor thinking she might have the flu. The doctor gave her a shot and sent them home. But Cristina didn't get any better, and Vicki felt uneasy. The baby's condition worsened, and she was rapidly losing weight.

One morning, Vicki went into the nursery to check on her and found Cristina covered in vomit and diarrhea. She rushed her to the hospital. Vicki held Cristina close, praying for God to heal her baby girl. But it was not to be. Cristina looked up into her mommy's eyes one last time, and then her spirit quietly left her. The doctors tried to revive the infant for forty-five minutes, but her little heart wouldn't start again. Cristina was only five months and three days old. Gary arrived at the hospital and heard the tragic news.

Completely devastated, Vicki sought answers from the doctor. The doctor first blamed Vicki, the young mother, for the illness of her child. She knew Cristina had been a well cared for baby and couldn't understand how he could accuse her of neglect. Such thoughts were more than she could bear. Then the autopsy report came back. Cristina had a rare intestinal disorder—the doctors just didn't know in time to save her life.

Vicki couldn't eat or sleep. The tears kept flowing, and depression took hold. The pain was so intense. Vicki felt paralyzed by grief. Cristina was the little girl she had always dreamed of having. Why had God taken her away? Was it cruel punishment for her sin? What was she supposed to learn through this trial? How would Gary ever become a believer now, knowing God had not saved his child? Vicki distanced herself from her friends and family, enclosing herself in the deep sorrow that she felt no one could understand. She couldn't bring herself to go to Cristina's funeral. It was too final.

Finally, with strength to do nothing else, Vicki began to immerse herself in the Bible. "Never will I leave you; / never will I forsake you" rang in her ears (Heb. 13:5). She wanted to believe His promise that "all things work together for good" (see Rom. 8:28). Visits from her faithful Sunday school teacher offered her healing and comfort. This woman came and prayed with Vicki anytime Vicki called, sometimes at three in the morning. Gary saw the woman's faithfulness and her deep love for Jesus. Seeds were being planted in his heart. Vicki continued to cling to her Bible for strength. Slowly, God strengthened the young mother through the grieving process.

Eventually, Vicki and Gary decided to try to have another child. As soon as Vicki learned she was pregnant, her hope was renewed. On December 8, 1971, Timothy was born. Vicki felt the blessing of having another child, and the cloud of depression lifted.

Looking back, Vicki knows that God used Cristina's short time on earth to teach her and Gary more about God's love. Through the time of suffering and loss, Gary came to know the Lord. He saw Cristina as the little one who led him to Christ. After losing her daughter, Vicki became more determined to give God everything within her—all of her life. The couple grew closer in their marriage, committed to God and each other.

Vicki, now the proud mom of two sons, counsels others in her church who are enduring similar circumstances. She knows that God is using her trials to strengthen others.

God is light; in him there is no darkness at all. If we claim to have fellowship with him yet walk in the darkness, we lie and do not live by the truth. But if we walk in the light, as he is in the light, we have fellowship with one another, and the blood of Jesus, His Son, purifies us from all sin.

(1 John 1:5–7)

jane elder
THE POWER OF YES

Jane Elder was born in the tiny bayside town of Palacios, Texas, shortly after the turn of the twentieth century. Rough Rider Teddy Roosevelt was president of the United States, and horses and buggies still outnumbered automobiles. The San Andreas fault line in California was silently shifting toward the great earthquake of 1906 that would rock the city of San Francisco just days after Jane's birth.

She was the eighth of nine children, born to a forty-year-old mother who was widowed just four short years later. Jane insisted that the most remarkable thing about her life was its length, but the impact she made for Christ in her ninety years was what really made her stand out.

Jane's life hinged on the power of a simple *yes* spoken when she was twelve years old. She recalls that a traveling evangelist had come to their town, and his message touched her heart: "I was a kid who grew up around the water—swimming, diving, and all. And he told this story about a father who got in the water and told his child to jump, and that he would catch him. When the child hesitated, the father said, 'You know, you can trust your daddy. Just trust me and jump.' When he spoke those words, I felt the Lord convict me, and I was saved."

Jane later joked that her baptism in Palacios Bay was no geographical coincidence, but an absolute necessity: "I was so mean it took plenty of saltwater to clean me up. Regular water wouldn't do," she said with a twinkle in her eye.

Just a short time later, she attended a youth meeting where her *yes* to Jesus Christ became *yes* to whatever He might have planned for her still-young life. "[The congregation was] singing, 'I'll go where You want me to go, dear Lord, / on mountain or plain or sea. / I'll do what You want me to do, dear Lord; / I'll be what You want me to be.' And that's when I stepped out and took the preacher's hand and said that the message of that song was for me. I didn't know what a little girl from Palacios could do, but whatever it was, I decided to do it."

Jane's *yes* began a seventy-eight-year stretch of teaching in whatever church she served. She began teaching the Bible to kindergartners when she was thirteen, and throughout her life she taught single women, young brides, and older married women the truths she faithfully gleaned from God's Word. In later years she led an elderly group of women called the Mary Marthas, who were sometimes joined by what Jane referred to as "the occasional Lazarus"—an aging husband accompanying his wife to Sunday school, or a widower who ambled in and made himself at home.

Throughout her years of teaching, although she taught every book of the Bible several times over, Jane never repeated a lesson. "I don't ever save an outline," she remembered, "because I think you should study fresh for every lesson. And we don't teach a lesson—we teach people." Not only did she teach new lessons every class, she was certain that the chief advantage to all those years of study was hers: "It's always the teacher who gains the most," she said.

Although she lost her father at such a young age that she barely remembered him and had her share of sweethearts but never married, Jane's life was deeply intertwined with two very special men of God. The first, Dr. F. B. Thorne, pastored churches in Houston, Texas, and Wichita, Kansas, in the 1930s and 1940s. In 1933, Dr. Thorne called Jane in Dallas, where she worked for the state Baptist headquarters, and asked her to come work for him in Houston's Second Baptist Church—a young, growing congregation that was heavily in debt.

She remembered, "It was during the Depression, and I was afraid to leave my job, but you see, I'd said yes all those years before, and so I did. In April of 1933, I met my new boss, and I worked for him for twenty-nine years." Jane served Dr. Thorne in Houston and in Wichita, and after his death she cared for his wife until Mrs. Thorne passed away at the age of eighty-four.

After Mrs. Thorne's death, Jane returned to Houston and the church she'd served with Dr. Thorne. She was then at an age when most people were planning their retirement, but she continued working tirelessly for the Lord. When her church found itself without a leader in the 1970s, she sat on the committee to select a new pastor.

Her assignment lasted nearly three years and required ninety-seven committee meetings, 147 interviews, and hundreds of thousands of miles logged to find the right man. Ed Young of Columbia, South Carolina, was nominated and unanimously voted in as the fifth pastor of Second Baptist

Church. Soon after, Jane's phone rang, and her new pastor asked her to come and serve her church again—that time as director of missions.

"Do you know how old I am?" she asked him.

"I do," he said, "and if you were any younger, I wouldn't want you."

"I want to play a while," she told him. "I've worked so many years, I just want to take a break."

"Play all you want to," he told her. "Your salary's going to start the first of next month."

So once again, the little girl from Palacios said yes. And in the final twenty years of her life, Jane Elder taught, raised nearly $8 million for missions in Houston and abroad, and answered every call for duty from the church she loved. She went in to work every day and never missed a worship service. She worked circles around men and women half her age. When illness put her in the hospital for the last time, a steady stream of pastors came to pray for her healing—until she told them to stop.

"Miss Jane," one of them told her, "you've got to get well! We need you up at the church."

She lifted her oxygen mask off her face, shook her head firmly, and said, "No. I'm going home."

Someone asked one of the pastors who visited her at the end, "How did she look?"

"Like a girl getting ready for the biggest date of her life," he said with a smile.

At her funeral service, the pastor who'd been like a son to her summed up her life: "Did Jane Elder have gifts that were superior to those of other people? Not at all. I think Jane was a garden-variety, ordinary, normally gifted Palacios girl who at one moment in her life said, 'Lord, I surrender all.' And the difference was she really *did* surrender. She really did give her all. And she didn't hold anything back."

Jane Edler said yes. She meant it. Few experience the extraordinary power of a heartfelt *yes*.

The fruit of the Spirit is love, joy, peace, patience, kindness, goodness, faithfulness, gentleness, and self control. Against such things there is no law.

(Galatians 5:22–23)

WEEK ELEVEN JOURNAL

—◆—

⇒ What does peace look like in the life of a believer?

⇒ If you could have that peace in one area of your life, which would it be?

⇒ What are the most difficult issues you've had to face in your life?

⇒ How can your stories of difficulty and struggle be molded into a message of hope for others?

⇒ What Bible verse or passage of Scripture has been most meaningful to you this week? Why?

nisha

DANGER EVERY DAY

The sun was high and the streets of the village were crowded when the angry mob burst into fifteen-year-old Nisha's home. Her father and brothers were at work, so no one was there to protect Nisha and her mother from the men who grabbed them and forced them outside.

Nisha clutched her sari as she was dragged down the packed earth streets of Kilipala, the Indian village where she lived. She saw other women being pulled from their homes and recognized them as members of her small Christian church. She knew her attackers as well; some of them were her neighbors. A few were relatives of the women being abducted. All of the men were religious Hindus.

The mob gathered their victims—seven women, including Nisha and another teenage girl, and their Christian pastor, Subash Samal—in a central part of the village. A leader stepped forward from the circle of angry faces and addressed the frightened women. He told them that they could not be Christians anymore. He told them about the "evils of Christianity." Nisha recognized his words as similar to those spread through the village recently by extremist Hindu groups.

There are not many Christians in the poor, mostly illiterate Indian state of Orissa, and those who do live there are often abused. Thirteen people were killed and more than 150 homes were destroyed across the region in 1999 during anti-Christian riots. Many cases of physical violence against Christians have been reported every year since then.

In Kilipala, relationships between Hindus and Christians had not always been so bad. But tensions had flared recently when two girls from Hindu families started attending Pastor Samal's church. Their parents tried to force them to convert back to Hinduism, but they refused and moved out of their families' homes.

Indian law prevents any religion from "forcing conversion"—in fact, a person must fill out paperwork with the government before he or she is allowed to change religions—so the families reported Pastor Samal to the police. The innocent man produced legal affidavits signed by the girls in question, showing that they made their own choices to become Christians.

Some of the extremists in Kilipala were still upset, though, and during the first week of February 2004, a crowd rounded up the pastor and the Christian women of the town. The Hindus wanted to punish these followers of a foreign religion for taking people away from what they saw as the true Indian faith.

The crowd demanded that Nisha and the other Christian women convert back to Hinduism. Most of the Christians in Kilipala had accepted Christ more than seven years before, so they were not new believers. They were confident in their faith, and they believed in eternal salvation through Jesus

Christ. One by one, each woman refused to renounce her Christianity.

The mob became violent and beat the Christians. If a woman fought back, they stripped off her clothes and forced her to stand naked in front of everyone. When the angry, strong men turned to her, Nisha considered denying Christ and agreeing to become a Hindu. But she remembered what she had learned about the apostle Peter, who denied Jesus on the night that He was arrested. Could she do that, after what Christ had suffered for her? No, Nisha was a Christian. She endured her beating in silence; she would not renounce Christ.

Battered and naked, the women continued to defend their Christian faith. The Hindus were enraged; if the women would not reconvert to Hinduism, then at least they would look as if they had!

One of the men stepped forward with a razor, and Nisha began to cry. He grabbed one of the women closest to him and roughly shaved all of the hair from the crown of her head. This was called tonsuring, and in India, it was the religious symbol of a Hindu convert. It is a severe insult to many in India to be a Christian and tonsured.

The man violently shaved the heads of each woman and then the pastor. Only one—Lata, who was pregnant—he left alone.

Eventually, the mob's anger faded, and the women were allowed to leave. Nisha and her mother returned to their home, shaking and humiliated.

Nisha knew she could not stay in Kilipala after what had happened to her. She could not show her raw, shaved head in public. She could not see the neighbors, the relatives who had done this to her. Nisha did not trust the police in the area to punish the men for what they had done. Crimes against Christians were rarely prosecuted.

When her father returned home and found out what happened, he told Nisha to pack her things. Fearing a greater retaliation for the women's refusal to convert, Nisha's family joined twenty other Christians as they fled to Orissa's state capital of Bhubaneshwar. It was a bigger city with a larger Christian population. Nisha's family prayed that the churches there could protect them.

The Kilipala Christians found refuge at the Church of Mount Zion, where they stayed for several months waiting for the violence to subside. When Nisha and the other women first tried to report the incident to the police, some of the officers refused even to file their complaint. Finally, the women were allowed to report the names of thirty-five men who had attacked them. It took months—and the intervention of the national court system—before six of the men were arrested. That same week, Pastor Samal was also detained, apparently for allowing himself to be forcibly converted.

Nisha and her family have finally returned to Kilipala. They have found a changed town, full of increased suspicion and violence. Although they had been the victims of the attack, not the aggressors, some of their Hindu neighbors seem to blame them for what had happened. Crowds sometimes gather to prevent Nisha and the other Christian women from drawing fresh drinking water at the local well. Pastor Samal has been arrested again and again on false charges.

Yet Nisha and the rest of the Christian community in Kilipala, India, continue to defend their faith, despite the persecution. They face scorn and danger every day for the sake of one who also faced scorn and danger. They stand as a testimony of Christian commitment and an example of real sacrifice.

Then Jesus came to them and said, "All authority in heaven and on earth has been given to me. Therefore go and make disciples of all nations, baptizing them in the name of the Father and of the Son and of the Holy Spirit, and teaching them to obey everything I have commanded you. And surely I am with you always, to the very end of the age."

(Matthew 28:18–20)

renata rodriques oliveira
SENT BY GOD

When Renata was eighteen, she left her family's home on the southern coast of Brazil to serve as a missionary in nearby Curitiba. Although she knew God had called her to share the gospel, Renata had no idea what obeying Him would mean.

For three years, Renata supported other Christians at a local Youth With a Mission base in Brazil. She was happy there, content to do what God wanted while deepening her own spiritual life. But in the summer of 2001, Renata heard about a group of Brazilian missionaries in Moscow who were seriously injured in a car accident.

Renata prayed for the health of the missionaries, who had once worked at the Curitiba base, and for the survival of their program. Russia had outlawed Christianity for decades under Communism, and Renata knew there weren't many mature Christians left in the country to help build local churches and train Russian Christian leaders. She was troubled to hear that the Discipleship Training School (DTS) where the Brazilian missionaries worked was so understaffed that it might have to close. Her own mission in Brazil was overstaffed. "It did not make sense to close something for lack of people to help if in another part [of the world] we had people in excess," she explains.

Like the prophet Isaiah, Renata heard God asking, "Whom shall I send? And who will go for us?" (6:8). She began to pray about moving to Russia to serve with the mission team. It was a frightening idea—it would cost thousands of dollars. Renata had never left Brazil, much less traveled to the opposite side of the globe. She would have to adjust to a new climate and language, and the monthly support required to live in a European country was five times what she needed in Brazil. Renata struggled, but after careful prayer and study, she knew it was what God wanted her to do. She was content to serve Him in Brazil, but she found she was passionate about serving Him in Russia. She was excited to answer His call: "Here I am, Lord, send me."

Her departure for Russia was truly a miracle itself. In only twenty-three days, she raised the money she needed to make the trip. Her paperwork came through, and a plane ticket was arranged.

When Renata arrived in Moscow, the overworked mission staff received her gratefully. She settled into her new routine, soon realizing how difficult the language barrier could be in her ministry. Renata knew no Russian, and none of the Russian students in the program knew Portuguese. Yet almost 80 percent of Renata's work required her to communicate with the students. While other missionaries were sometimes available to act as translators, Renata and her students often resorted to a paper and pencil, drawing cartoon-like sketches to illustrate ideas.

After six months in the Moscow base, the Discipleship Training School students prepared for two months of evangelism work across Russia. Renata watched and helped them get ready, but she was content to stay behind. Her Russian language skills were still rough, and she didn't know nearly enough to get by in the country.

God is not limited by language, though, and once again, He called Renata to be more than just content. The Brazilian girl was shocked when her DTS director asked her not only to attend the evangelism program, but to lead a team of students going to southern Russia.

For the first time since she had answered the call to missions, Renata wanted to turn down an assignment. She asked the director for time to pray about the opportunity, and then went to God to explain why she was not qualified for this. "I am limited, Lord," she told Him. "I can only go so far, and beyond that it's not possible. I need to recognize my limits."

As soon as she heard her own excuses, though, Renata knew God's answer. "It is true. You are really a limited person. You have a great barrier in your way. But Renata, do not make your limits My limits, because I don't have them. For Me, there are no barriers."

Renata knew she was called to lead the Russian students, and despite her own fears, she chose to obey God. As she boarded a train, exchanging nervous smiles with her five Russian-speaking charges, Renata's fright almost made her turn back.

But she didn't, and the girls on her team were patient and eager to help her learn. After a few weeks, Renata began to feel she could share the gospel with Russians.

On a bitterly cold autumn day, Renata and her team were hanging out near a train station, hoping to witness to people as they passed by. Unfortunately, it was so cold that almost no one was on the street that day. When the six girls saw an older man walking a few yards away from them, they all ran toward him, eager for someone to whom they might talk.

The man was homeless; he clutched his belongings in a plastic bag and looked silently at each girl as she spoke. When he looked at Renata, his eyes were kind, and for the first time she felt confident in her ability to speak Russian. Renata used every word she knew to tell him about Jesus. The old man never furrowed his brow or looked confused, the way many Russians did when they didn't understand Renata. Instead, he watched her attentively and expressed approval with his eyes. *This is it,* she thought. She was getting through!

Renata's confidence was short-lived. After a few moments, the man interrupted with a gesture and began apologetically pointing to his ears. He was deaf. He hadn't understood a single thing Renata said.

Disappointed, the girls pantomimed their message—that Jesus loved the man and wanted to help him—and gave him a copy of the New Testament with their church information in the back. The gentle beggar bowed his head and touched his heart to show his gratitude. But for Renata, as she walked away, the encounter was a failure. Once again, she had not been able to tell a person about the message of salvation. Renata felt empty and useless. There she was, halfway around the world, and she had nothing to offer.

That week, Renata and her team spoke to many people on the streets of the small city. Many of them seemed to understand Renata's Russian and expressed interest in her message; she began to feel confident in her calling again.

In church that Sunday, Renata looked around to see if anyone she spoke to the week before had come. To her shock, she recognized only the deaf beggar. Why was he there, if he had not understood what the girls told him? And where was everyone else from the week? Where were the people who had heard her words?

Renata felt God speaking to her heart once again. "The difference between the homeless man and the people who did not come is not in what you have done. I am the one who makes the difference. You trust more in yourself and in what you can do than in My power. I just need you to be willing."

That time, the message clicked. God called Renata to be willing to go to Russia, but He made it happen. He called her to be willing to travel to southern Russia to evangelize, but He brought the people to her. And He called her to be willing to talk to a cold, homeless, deaf man, but He made the beggar understand. It wasn't about her abilities; it was about her willingness to obey.

Despite the discomfort of a foreign country and language, Renata Rodrigues Oliveira let God work through her to accomplish His purposes; her obedience, rather than her talents, continues to change the lives of many Christians in Russia today.

Be wise in the way you act toward outsiders; make the most of every opportunity. Let your conversation be always full of grace, seasoned with salt, so that you may know how to answer everyone.

(Colossians 4:5–6)

мary carol мazza
MOVING FORWARD IN FAITH

A stranger might look at Mary Carol Mazza's résumé and wonder if she knows what it is she's after. But anyone who meets this vibrant, brilliant twenty-four-year-old quickly learns that the answer is simple, really: she wants to follow her God wherever He is leading.

So far, He has led her to a joint degree in economics and psychology from Virginia's prestigious Washington and Lee University, a season of study in Austria, a stint as a summer camp counselor in Oregon, a policy job at the Texas Department of Health & Human Services, a summer at a women and children's shelter in New York City, and missions work in Bolivia, Brazil, and Eastern Asia.

And she's just getting started.

An only child who grew up attending a private Christian school in Houston, Texas, Mary Carol came to know Jesus Christ at a young age. Her mother shares her faith, but her father does not.

"I've prayed since I was in fifth grade that my dad would know Christ," she says. "My family has always been divided in that way, and it's caused a kind of split in my heart that I've carried since junior high. A lot of the choices I've made don't seem reasonable to my dad. He wants me to do what to him would be the sensible thing: go to law school, settle down, and have a successful career using the gifts I've been given. And maybe it *is* easier to just please other people and do what's expected of you. But there's nothing better than following God in faith—seeing the way He leads and the things He does—and being able to say, 'God did that!' That's the only way for me."

If there was ever any question, a turning point for Mary Carol was probably the summer between her sophomore and junior years in college; she spent eight weeks living as an intern at a women's shelter in Queens, New York. "All my friends were interning on Wall Street," she remembers. "And when we'd meet up in the city they'd be talking about all the great stuff they were involved in, and say, 'Now *what* is it you're doing?'"

What she was doing was whatever it took to befriend and assist the residents of the shelter. "Some days it might be getting milk for their kids. Or just sitting on the side of a bed and listening to someone's story. "I started organizing little outings for the residents. I was 'that crazy girl from Texas' who said, 'Hey, let's all go to the Brooklyn Botanical Gardens this week. It's free on Wednesdays!' The amazing thing was, some of them actually did!"

Many of the women she lived with that summer were abused, addicted, and angry. Being in the middle of so much pain was a far cry from attending the sheltered, white-columned university just a few hours away. "I felt overwhelmed at times by their situations and their needs. It was lonely and scary, and

I truly felt that God was all I had," Mary Carol says. "I was there to build relationships, but they were pretty skeptical at first. When they saw that I wasn't going anywhere, things began to change. What I was doing seemed small compared to [what] some of my friends [were doing], but it was incredibly fulfilling to me."

The experience in New York solidified her desire to help others and taught her that building relationships was much more important than just offering detached service. That passion for involvement carried over to activities on campus, where she discipled other female undergrads through her dorm and sorority. "My senior year at W & L was all about relationships. It wasn't about getting into a graduate program or getting a fellowship or landing a great job."

As she began to invest in the lives of others, she saw a proliferation of women with whom she did share something in common: eating disorders that were hidden but powerful and disruptive. "It's rampant on campus," says Mary Carol. "And I thought, *I'm a psychology major—I'm going to do something about this.*" She and a few other women took on a research project on anorexia and bulimia, interviewing students and sharing their findings. "We began to speak out about the problem to other girls, trying to bring it out into the open," she says. "We figured we need to talk about this stuff and not keep it a secret. We need to figure out how to heal."

There was also a special relationship for Mary Carol at W & L—an undergraduate named Andy, two years her junior, who became a close friend, and then a boyfriend. They clicked almost immediately but had been dating only a short time when Mary Carol felt a nudge from God to pull back. They cared for one another deeply but agreed that the timing wasn't right. "I haven't really spoken with him in over a year," she says, "but I'm trusting God to bring us together again if that's what He desires. It's hard to let go, but God has our very best in mind, and I'm trusting in His timing. I know this is His will right now, and I'm settled in it."

Mary Carol moved to Austin after graduation and found herself challenged and stretched by her job at the Texas Department of Health & Human Services, taking part in an investigation of the state's Child Protective Services agency. She found a church in Austin and became involved there, but after a little more than a year, she felt the tug of God's leading again, this time to a kind of spiritual hiatus that may be her biggest challenge yet. She's heading to Nashville, Tennessee, for an extended stay at Mercy Ministries, where she'll open her heart and seek God's healing for the "thorn" that's been lodged there for years: her eating disorder.

"I believe God is calling me to do something big for Him, and I need to get ready. This is an area of my life that I know I need to work on. I don't want to be weighed down by it any-more—or carry it into my marriage or pass it on to my chil-dren. God wants me whole, and He's calling me away for a while to settle some things with Him."

To some it may seem like a detour, but Mary Carol knows otherwise. "I've had enough experience to know when God is leading," she says, "and to know that I want to follow. Maybe 'big' for me will be to get married and have a family. Or maybe it will be to move overseas and do missions work. Maybe I'll go back to my job in Austin and He'll have another assignment for me there, but I'm in preparation for the life He's planned for me. There's nothing more important now than deepening my relationship with the Lord—because that's what we'll be doing for eternity. God is teaching me that obedience does not require understanding. His question is simply, 'Will you follow Me?' and I mean for my answer to be 'Yes!'"

To all who received him, to those who believed in his name, he gave the right to become children of God.

(John 1:12)

---

lori jo
LOVE CHILD

From birth Lori Jo has been two distinct people: the spunky and caring daughter of a preacher and a rebel and independent bent on threshing her own trail. Lori Jo was practically born in a pew, and in the eyes of her parents she was their star child. Teachers raved about her "wisdom beyond years," friends were never hard to come by, and Lori was a coach's pet due to her love of sports and natural talent to perform on the field and court. Still, she's always tried to hide behind her abilities, preferring not to be noticed; she has feared what people would see in her if they looked too close: a hypocrite.

The summer before Lori Jo entered sixth grade, her parents told her the family was moving to the Great Northwest. Oregon? Lori Jo couldn't move there. She was going to attend the University of Arizona with her friends; she was going to marry Kelton Busby, the Mormon boy she adored; and she had just moved up to be a senior league shortstop.

After their first year up in "God's country," as Lori Jo's dad so gleefully called it, she began to warm up—or more like thaw out. She met new friends, was given a horse, and lived amid beautiful mountain trails that she climbed on her new bike. Lori Jo had also found the perfect spot to smoke menthol cigarettes where she could keep a vigilant eye on who came and went from her house.

Lori Jo kept church friends fenced off from school friends. She couldn't very well be the same LJ with the young Bible beaters that she was at school. Again, she artfully created two lives, the rebel and the preacher's daughter. You could say Lori Jo had a healthy aversion to the "churchy," uptight, saintly types. They only reminded her of what she could not (and did not) want to be. Lori Jo was skeptical of and distant from many who claimed to follow the same Christ she did. They made it look too easy.

Her introduction to marijuana took place when she was fifteen. From her first puff, Lori Jo was hooked on getting high from weed grown in "God's country." She was popular in more than one circle and was soon connected with the best marijuana the area had to offer.

One of Lori Jo's first experiences with alcohol is unforgettable. En route to a family reunion, she and her parents spent a couple of days in Southern California, where Lori Jo hung out with her older cousin. The cousin thought it would be cool to sneak Lori Jo out of the North American Christian Convention and into a bar where her boyfriend was gambling away his paycheck. Although Lori Jo could smoke joints with the best of them, she was far from a seasoned drinker like the three towering ASU basketball players with whom her cousin left her.

Time warped, and when Lori Jo came to and opened her eyes, it was to find herself under the weight of a really big guy. Her neck was being rammed up against a hard, sharp surface behind her. She had no idea where she was or why the guy who had been sitting across from her was now on top of her. Lori Jo couldn't recall leaving the bar, entering the camper, or giving the go-ahead to take her virginity. From that night forward, her guilt knew no end. It wasn't until years later, when she finally let the story out, that she was assured she'd been raped.

Lori Jo shut down and remained closed to those church folk around her who still believed she was a *love child*—a child of God. Instead, she retreated to a place where drugs and promiscuous relationships made life more surreal and bearable. After that night, Lori Jo shut out her family from her private life for many, many years.

By the time she was seventeen, she was very comfortable using cigarettes, pot, alcohol, acid, mushrooms, cocaine, methamphetamines, and heroin. Buying and selling were old hat by Lori Jo's sophomore year, and she even began growing "the special herb" in her bedroom near the end of high school. Drugs became her focus, her priority, for four years. Still, she somehow managed to pull good grades, play sports, remain popular among various cliques, participate in church events, and remain extremely active in outdoor activities.

As long as Lori Jo was high, she didn't have to face who she had become—how low she had stooped. She didn't have to think about how she was going to quit that lifestyle and start fresh, drug free, sex free . . . clean. Her guilt and shame were made worse by the voice inside her that continually whispered, "You are My love child, I made you, I love you!" Lori Jo knew if she believed that voice, it meant she would have to give up control of her life and return to the place she knew she belonged.

But in the end God's love was too great for her to ignore. The semester before Lori Jo graduated from high school, she became the first person in the local day-treatment program to sign herself up. It was a sober summer and she felt great, ready to start fresh with the help of her new grip on faith. Lori Jo told her parents about everything except her lost virginity and list of unnamed boyfriends. She would not be ready to open that box for many years to come.

Everything looked great right up until college started. The day before she left for L.A., she freaked out and packed some speed in her bag to help ease the transition from "hippy chick" to "straight sister." The drugs kept Lori Jo up the entire first week of school. She let fear overcome what she knew was true—that living within her she had a Power greater than any drug. The Holy Spirit was there to help her walk through the awkwardness of joining her new "straight and narrow" community. After seven sleepless nights, Lori Jo finally realized she no longer wanted nor needed the tricks in her bag, and she threw them out for good. Lori Jo truly wanted to let God lead her and show her a better way.

Lori Jo would like to say that Christian college was exactly what she needed, that she changed all her old habits and became a shining example of obedience. Although her years there definitely helped in her formation, Lori Jo was hardly transformed into the cover girl for *Christian Woman Today*. She learned that simply creating space for God was half the battle. She also discovered that she wasn't the only one struggling with her spiritual journey. Still, Lori Jo constantly felt condemned as a hypocrite because she could not swear off cigarettes and an occasional mellow high while sitting on her balcony or lying on the beach.

Lori Jo doesn't downplay the wayward choices that demonstrated time and again her incapacity to live out her faith consistently. The fact is she began to learn more about the character of God, and as she did, she began seeing herself as

He does. Lori Jo could see how a light was beginning to shine in her eyes where years of drug and relational abuse had dulled and shaded her sight. She started to believe she was blessed, one who had something to give others: a gift of forgiveness and acceptance. Escaping with drugs began to lose its influence and in quiet moments of meditation, Lori Jo began to faintly hear again her Father's words, "You are My love child."

Granted, there were moments when she completely lost it and felt like a lunatic. Was she growing or merely spinning in circles? Why couldn't she see the person others saw her becoming? She sometimes stayed up all night, smoking cigarettes and drinking wine, while completing a reading assignment for Bible class.

Then came the other moments when she caught glimpses of what God was shaping and molding her for, moments of surrender to her Creator. Those times always came when Lori Jo was serving the poor, the broken, and those who had slipped through the holes of the web that so snugly sought to hold her safe. Perhaps she had found an avenue by which to love her own broken spirit—by investing in those "undeserving" folks. The mystery continues to intrigue her.

Two years ago, God's quiet voice again beckoned Lori Jo, this time to serve the people of South America. She said yes (with much fear and doubt) and has since felt blessings and adventures heaped upon her. She was then invited to join her new Latin community to participate in a humanitarian aide pilot team in Iraq during the U.S.-led war.

So, nearly a year ago, hauling a backpack and an acoustic guitar, Lori Jo boarded a plane headed for Iraq (the world's most undesirable and perilous vacation destination at that moment). Showing slight trepidation and possessing nothing more than a round-trip plane ticket, she began what continues to be the journey of a lifetime. During the past eight months she's been granted a dream: Lori Jo has designed a women's complex where international and local staff will meet the needs of thousands of women.

In the end, the decision to move to Iraq was prompted by Lori Jo's desire to know more deeply one outstanding mystery—one that reverberates with each beat of her heart, one she remains intrigued by and somehow convinced of to this day: "To live is Christ and to die is gain" (Phil. 1:21).

Lori Jo still battles with the voices in her head that tell her she will never be clean or good enough to deserve what the Scriptures say her Creator wants for her. But the truth remains: before anyone named her, touched her, or defined her, Lori Jo was His. He chose her and when she was yet a sinner, Christ died for her (see Rom. 5:8). She continues to take one step at a time on the Jesus Trail.

Sometimes they are sidesteps, at other times leaps forward, and sometimes steps backward. Lori Jo is amazed at how far she once tried to run from this love, this path of grace, just to find herself right where she began.

Yes, Lori Jo is a love child. She says she's still a hippy chick, but she's following His lead and He's bringing her closer and closer to what He designed her to be: a creaky, twisted, broken . . . beautiful conduit of His love.

———— · ———— · ———— · ———— · ———— · ————

How great is the love the Father has lavished on us, that we should be called the children of God! And that is what we are!

(1 John 3:1)

———— · ———— · ———— · ———— · ———— · ————

rebekah tauber
GOD'S ODD GIFT

The last six months have been the hardest of seventeen-year-old Rebekah Tauber's life. But she just might tell you they have also been the best.

In the spring semester of her sophomore year, Rebekah was feeling great and loving life and school when she noticed a swollen spot on her neck. Her pediatrician took a look and said it was probably nothing to worry about. Then came a few more doctors' appointments and a few more tests with no conclusive results. No one seemed to believe there was great cause for alarm, but Rebekah felt uneasy. She suspected that something might really be wrong.

A short time later, one doctor recommended a biopsy of the lump on her neck, and within a matter of days she was diagnosed with a rare form of soft-tissue cancer called rhabdomyosarcoma.

"As soon as I heard the word 'cancer,' all I could think of was losing my hair," she says. It didn't occur to her at first that she might be in for the fight of her life.

Rhabdomyosarcoma is diagnosed in only about 350 patients under the age of twenty each year. A majority of those children will survive with proper treatment—and the odds continue to improve. Rebekah's doctor at M.D. Anderson Cancer Center in Houston has been a leader in the study and treatment of the disease. She calls him "just about the smartest man alive," and with his help, she plans to enter her senior year of high school strong and cancer-free.

After surgery to remove her tumor and assess the spread of the disease, Rebekah began a rugged regimen of radiation and chemotherapy that has now become routine. She knows which days of the cycle are wearying, which will bring pain, which could mean a spike of fever, and which might actually be her "good days."

"Knowing the schedule and what will happen when is kind of comforting," she says, sitting on her hospital bed on the first day of a regular chemotherapy session. "And this place is starting to feel like a home away from home."

Each time she goes to the hospital for treatment, Rebekah brings a favorite pillow and a cozy fleece blanket a friend made. In her faded San Diego Padres T-shirt and flannel pajama pants, she could be any seventeen-year-old at a slumber party—except she's at least twenty pounds lighter than she was just a few months ago, and there's almost no hair on her head. And instead of giggling with other girls her age, she hangs out in her room with her mom or dad.

Sometimes friends drop in, like the four-year-old she met on a previous chemo trip, who pushes her plastic car up to the door of Rebekah's room while her mom pulls along an IV pole. "She wanted to come and see you," says the mother of the perfectly bald little girl. Rebekah, curled up in bed with her pillow and blanket, lights up in a smile and throws her arms open wide. It's a fellowship of survivors, and love flows unchecked.

For Rebekah, cancer has been less a rude interruption than an unexpected but welcome gift from God. "I've learned so much from cancer," she says. "I always depended on other people before. I went to church every Sunday, but the walk I had was not the walk I wanted. I depended on my friends first, before God—but not anymore. My friends are great, and they care about me, but they couldn't really understand what it was like to be sick. And I realized they couldn't make me happy anymore. In normal situations maybe they could help, but with this, God is the only one who really knows and understands, and He's the one who helps me."

While some of her friendships have become stronger through her illness, Rebekah admits that others are changing. "I'm growing closer to God through this," she says, "and there are some people who just don't understand that. Because of it, we don't have that much in common anymore, but it's okay."

Cancer has positively impacted even her relationships within her family. "My parents and I have become a lot closer," says Rebekah. "I really look up to them a lot. My mom is my best friend. Before I got sick I used to argue with her every single day, and I wasn't even home that much—but now we're together a lot, and when I'm home, our house is the house that everyone hangs out at. My friends are over all the time, and they're close to my mom too. And my dad—well, one of the hardest things about all of this has been seeing my dad cry."

Rebekah's older brother David is a source of encouragement too. Though she says they didn't always get along well, "he wanted to skip his sophomore year at college so he could come home and be with me."

These days, love seems to be coming from every direction. "My mom said it best," Rebekah explains. "We're more used to being on the giving end than on the receiving end. But I get so much love and encouragement from other people. It's amazing to see people reach out and really care. I am so blessed."

Her church provided Rebekah with a pager, and word of how to use it to lift her spirits quickly spread. Friends and strangers alike call the pager number and leave their zip codes so she will know that someone is praying for her. The pager goes off so frequently that she's learned to keep it on "Vibrate," but the messages come in a steady stream almost all day, every day. "My dad has a special code he puts in so I'll know it's him," she says, "and my friends put their phone numbers in."

A close family friend sends regular e-mails to share prayer requests for Rebekah and pass along news of her recovery. Sometimes Rebekah writes back. One day she wrote:

I just thought I would share something small I've learned with everything I'm going through. I've realized that you honestly CAN NOT live without talking to God every day of your life. My friends and the people by my side may help, but they can't heal my hurt inside. But as soon as I talk to God or read the Bible, it's as if I'm a totally new person! When I talk to God I have so much joy and go from feeling empty to feeling completely filled—and even thankful for everything I'm going through.

Although she's working hard to get well, Rebekah is pretty certain she'd like to continue talking about the odd blessing of cancer whenever she can. "I want people to know that God doesn't make mistakes," she says with a smile. "Everything is the way it should be. God is there for you all the time. Trust Him. He's there. Pray to Him. He'll answer. I wouldn't have known these things without cancer, and I love telling people about what I've been through, and how God is helping me."

No temptation has seized you except what is common to man. And God is faithful; he will not let you be tempted beyond what you can bear. But when you are tempted, he will also prove a way out so that you can stand up under it.

(1 Corinthians 10:13)

WEEK TWELVE JOURNAL

＋═ When have you felt out of reach of God's love?

＋═ What does the Bible tell us about His love?

＋═ How does this affect your ability to love yourself? Others? God?

＋═ How do you see God using these stories to change your life?

＋═ What Bible verse or passage of Scripture has been most meaningful to you this week? Why?

⊰ authors' note ⊱

We authors would like to gratefully acknowledge the assistance of the many people who shared their stories with us. In particular, we want to say thanks to the good folks at Voice of the Martyrs, who put us in touch with many people and shared their stories.

If you'd like to be encouraged by the testimonies of today's persecuted Christians, or if you'd like to learn how you can pray more effectively for your brothers and sisters in restricted nations, please visit www.persecution.com or call Voice of the Martyrs at 800-747-0085. Their free newsletter will bring you into the hearts and minds of those who are persecuted for the cause of Christ, and you can discover practical ways to stand with them. *Your faith will never be the same!*

⚜ notes ⚜

Week Three, Day 3
1. Letter to several nuns by Martin Luther, from Wittenburg, 6 August 1524. Translated from Johann Georg Walch, ed., *Dr. Luther's Briefe*, Part 1, Vol. 21, Part 1 (St. Louis: Concordia Publishing House, 1903).

Week Eight, Day 5
1. Steve Blow, "Deadly Visit to Iraq Leaves No Regret," *Dallas Morning News*, July 18, 2004. Used by permission.

⊰ about the authors ⊱

Australian-born Rebecca St. James has throughout the '90s until the present had a defining presence in contemporary Christian music. With sales of her music soaring around the globe, her signature blend of modern pop/rock sensibilities and lyrics of unwavering devotion have blazed straight to the heart of an entire generation. A multiple Dove winner, her groundbreaking album *Pray* was certified gold by RIAA in 2005, joining earlier honors for *God*, which was also awarded America's highest musical award—the Grammy. With a career track that has to date included seventeen top-10 singles, nine of them reaching #1 on the charts, she has in the last few years also been recognized as a bestselling CBA author with major books such as *Wait For Me* and *SHE* to her credit. Often called the "voice of her generation" in modern media, her impact has been diversely felt from television appearances ranging from *Hannity & Colmes* to the *700 Club*. Rebecca St. James remains a passionate global spokeswoman for Compassion International children's ministry. Find out more about Rebecca at www.rsjames.com.

Mary E. DeMuth is a freelance writer and novelist who lives in Southern France with her husband and three children. In addition to speaking, leading Bible studies, and enjoying worship, Mary assists her husband in a new church plant, reaching out to the emerging culture in France. You can find out more about Mary at www.relevantprose.com.

Elizabeth Jusino is a freelance writer, editor, and fan of the English language, with a special passion for writing for and about women. She is the former editor of *MOMSense Magazine* and managing editor for MOPS (Mothers of Preschoolers) International. She and her husband, Eric, live in Denver, Colorado.

Tracey D. Lawrence is a freelance writer and founder of Scribe Ink, Inc., serving ministries and organizations with writing and curriculum needs. She has written for ministries such as Chuck Colson's BreakPoint, the Wilberforce Forum, Promise Keepers, and Focus on the Family. Her latest release is *Playing God: Facing Everyday Dilemmas of Biotechnology,* featuring Chuck Colson. She lives in Denver, Colorado, with her husband, Noel. Tracey can be reached at traceydlaw@aol.com.

Leigh McLeroy is the author of *Moments for Singles* (NavPress, 2004) and a contributor to seven books including *Romancing the Home, Everywhere I Go,* and *Been There, Done That, Now What?* An accomplished writer, speaker, and Bible teacher, Leigh makes her home in Houston, Texas.

Donna Wallace has spent thirteen years studying and teaching on university campuses. She is a licensed minister of education with a master's degree in theological studies, and she loves speaking, writing, and guiding retreats about intimacy and identity development. Donna has written a dozen books and has several more on the way. She and her family live in Bozeman, Montana.